Title: Unexposed Power of Prayer: A Practical Guide, to praying, believing, and having miracles happen.

ISBN: 978-0-620-92916-5

Author: Dr Clifford Stanley Ferguson

Publisher: Amazon – 2021
Headquarters location - Seattle, Washington, USA.

Amazon Encore, Amazon Crossing, Montlake Romance, Lake Union, Thomas & Mercer, 47North, Topple Books.

amazonpublishing.amazon.com

Abstract

A handbook is required for believers to understand the dynamics of prayer. Herein the basics of prayer, the understanding of answered and unanswered prayer, together with the principles of fasting, unfold. Miracles do happen, the Holy Spirit is real, and revival starts when believers learn to pray. Prayer is like anything else in life, if you ask and believe in the cause, you will receive, God does answer prayer.

KEY WORDS

Jesus Christ, Holy Spirit, Prayer, spiritual warfare, miracles, believer, revival, disciples, interpretation, wisdom, knowledge, discernment, testimony, answered prayer.

Endorsements

Dr Clifford Stanley Ferguson has written an excellent book on "The unexposed power of prayer" which is sure to enhance your walk with God. This is not just a book written from knowledge acquired through study, but it is birthed in a personal experience and personal testimony of consistently living a Spirit-filled, Spirit-led life. Over the years I have personally seen Dr Clifford Ferguson living out these precious truths that he has written in this book. Therefore, I recommend this book to every believer who desires a closer walk and more intimate relationship with God. Grab it! Absorb it! Apply it! Dive into these truths and see the change in your life.

Pastor Lorentz La Grange - *National Convener Pentecostal Protestant Church of South Africa and Senior Pastor Shalom Montana*

I want congratulate Dr. Cliff Ferguson on his insight in the setting of this book and releasing it to the church of Christ as a practical outcome in line with Biblical principles. He is well known for his excellent and complete research strategy and this work is no exception. Prayer is addressed from a Biblical perspective and I recommend it for personal use, as a means of bettering the communication between God and man, and to discover God's purpose and plan for us. This book reads easily, and it is written and packaged in a format aimed not only at academics and can also be of great value to the ordinary believer. This masterpiece is recommended as a workbook for any congregation where prayer is a passion and where people are to be equipped for service. 1Thesallonians 5:17 "PRAY WITHOUT CEASING".

Dr Pieter Uys – *Pentecostal Protestant Church Head Office and Senior Pastor Bronkhorstspruit.*

Foreword and Dedication

This book I dedicate to my late father and mother, Pastor Keith and Alison Ferguson. Their forty years of ministry taught me many lessons, took me on a journey of fasting and prayer from an early age. My parents believed in miracles, not superficially, but by living experiences with God. As a child I saw them pray and as siblings, six of us, me the eldest, we knew what my mother and father prayed for would happen.

Their Journey with us, through life has left us with one real lesson and that is what you pray for sincerely, you will get. My mother was a prayer warrior, soft in the spirit, but as hard as a mother could be on what was right or wrong. When she prayed, heaven turned to deliver on God's will. My father, he was my best friend, if I ever had ministry problems, he was my confidant who would listen and pray with me for solutions.

I encourage everyone who reads this book to run the race of faith, learn more about God by reading your Bible and praying more, knowing that by faith and prayer mountains are moved.

Contents

CHAPTER 1

Introduction

I would like to start this book about prayer by explaining that prayer has always been a communication channel with God. It is in no way different to how we communicate with our loved ones, although, because God is invisible, we tend to believe that our prayers are travelling miles before they are heard. Being mindful of course, that our God, the living triune, Father, Son and Holy Spirit is omnipresent through the Holy Spirit. God the Father, Son and Spirit is the creator of all life (Genesis 1 and John 1) and has chosen men and women to be called sons and daughters of God. The Epistle John calls us a chosen nation, a peculiar people, and if I may add, we are enlightened beings, through the Holy Spirit, by the saving power of the Lamb's blood, Jesus God's only son. So, being born into the family of

God, He enables this peculiar person to interact with God, in a most natural, and peculiar way.

Therefore, when we pray in whatever way, we release spiritual power that travels miles to and from the throne room of God in heaven, where Jesus and the Father are, to the ends of the earth where the Angelic are, back to our minds and spirit, where we dwell in the Holy Spirit's presence. Nevertheless, the speed at which we converse with God must be much faster than that of light. Even faster than our communication, I believe, is the power that is released in the spiritual realm once our prayers are answered. Thus, in my understanding, the answers to our prayers, return from the Word of God, Jesus, via the Father on the throne. This Godly communication triangle releases the power of the living truth among men and women, by the Holy Spirit, and in many cases the

Angelic, under the command of the Father to serve His own.

Questions about prayer

In line with being "peculiar" believers become instruments in the hands of God, through the Holy Spirit (1) to move mountains by faith as promised by Jesus in Matthew 21:21, and Mark 11:23. Yet, with all this Godly power available, how does prayer work for us in our day-to-day situations. The problem of the Church is, although it is seen by the world as peculiar, the Church does not live up to the amount of spiritual energy that could be set loose through the prayers of the righteous. Thus, I intend to answer questions that relate to the power of prayer. These eight questions I list for topical discussion:

Q1 – How, why, when and what did Jesus pray?

Q2 – What are the fundamentals of prayer?

Q3 – What is the actual work of prayer?

Q4 – How does fasting influence the power of prayer?

Q5 – Why are so many prayers unanswered?

Q6 – Why prayer becomes a ritual?

Q7 – How can prayer bring about revival?

Q8 – How does God move through prayer?

Whilst there is no substitute for prayer, one needs to understand that it is a day-to-day activity of a peculiar nation to derive Godly results. This Godly activity causes spiritual motion to unleash undefined power. However, as children of God we do not fathom it, see, or activate it. Thus, my aspiration is to use this book as a guide to unleash the power captivated in your future prayers.

In answering the eight questions throughout the book, you may find that scripture of relevance has been repeated, I have specifically done so to ensure that the context of scripture within the topic is elevated for the purpose of better understanding. Thus, my motive for quoting scripture throughout was to ensure that the Biblical truth remains evident.

My theological angle may also differ from works of other theologians because we are individuals, who all seek relevance in theology for a captive audience. This is to gain as much insight into the subject matter as possible. I have therefore combined my own experience and theological background into this book so that it can be used by pastors and believers to enrich their approach to prayer and its undefined potential.

In closing my introduction, I will be starting with an in-depth discussion on Jesus and prayer. Whilst Jesus was on earth, I believe his walk of life reflects well on the way we should fast and pray to receive the positive results we expect. Furthermore, each chapter exits with a short assignment which allows for the implementation of prayer strategies and actions that will lead to spiritual maturity.

CHAPTER 2 - Back to Basics

The biggest problem the Christian community has is not praying enough and here I refer to the Muslim and Jewish communities who pray about five times per day. Yet, this can also be misconstrued as ceremonial prayer cannot replace personal prayer, and this is what I mean to speak to. It is all about the basics of prayer. I have witnessed ceremonial prayer in the desert of Kuwait in 1997, where teams of workers drop tools at noon, kneel and pray as one unit. There is an extreme discipline amongst the Muslim followers in the Middle East. Nonetheless, I do not wish to compare Islam to Christianity, yet my plea to Christians is, make disciplined time to pray. Through prayer we will overcome difficulties, problems, trauma and even persecution, this is a basic prescript of the Old and New

Testament. This leads me to several questions:

1. What is prayer actually?
2. What is the best time to pray?
3. How often should one pray?
4. What may one pray for?
5. Can one be healed if one prays for oneself?
6. What about success and prosperity in prayer?
7. Can a Christian pray for the dead?
8. May I include animals in my prayer?

I will in this chapter use the Bible and other sources to explain and answer the questions in such a way that Biblical truths and answers are evident. When answering these questions, one must not be biased or misled by tradition or theological standing. Henceforth, it is my task to remain biblically cantered in the exposition of the basics of prayer. The answers to the questions I have listed follow and I hope they inspire you to pray more and that your prayer journey will be made less cumbersome.

What is prayer actually?

To define prayer, it would be best to bring the first conversations between God and man into the picture. God spoke to Adam and Eve in the Garden of Eden, by implication daily, in the cool of the evening (Genesis 3:8-10). Thus, the start of prayer was a specific conversation with God at a specific time of day. I find significance in the thought of God befriending Adam and Eve and meeting with them in person. However, after their fall into sin the attention of God seems to move from intimate to graceful. Yet one finds and intimacy of God with certain individuals like Enoch and I quote Genesis 5:23-24 (KJV)

"And all the days of Enoch were three hundred sixty and five years: And Enoch walked with God: and he was *not; for God took him*".

The intimate relationship between Enoch and God must have been so overwhelming, I reiterate "walking with God" meant a Godly relationship in conversation and action. This almost seems to be a replacement of Adam; the point is that there is no relationship without a means of conversation. In conversation I mean dialogue between two parties.

My next icon is Noah, again, although it seems not as intimate as with Enoch, God destroys almost an entire human race through his obedience. One should compare again the "walked with God" in Genesis 5:24 and my quotation of Noah walking with God in Genesis 6:8-9 (KJV)

"But Noah found grace in the eyes of the LORD. These are the generations of Noah: Noah was a just man and perfect in his generations, and Noah walked with God".

In this respect Noah found grace with God and again had an intimate relationship with him, so much so that the entire plan of the flood and his safekeeping was given to him by God.

This certainly implies conversation or dialogue with trust and harmony.

When studying the life of Abram, God changes his name when making a covenant with him about a human race Genesis 17:3-5 (KJV)

"And Abram fell on his face: and God talked with him, saying, as for me, behold, my covenant is with thee, and thou shalt be a father of many nations. Neither shall thy name any more be called Abram, but thy

name shall be Abraham; for a father of many nations have I made thee".

Yet again, one finds a kind of intimacy in the relationship between God and Abraham, look at God's conversations with him about Lot and his wife and the destruction of Sodom and Gomora in Genesis 19. By 2019 the earth's occupancy is 7.7 billion (2) from early mathematical estimations of around five million (3) in the Abrahamic age. This is a direct indication of the favour of God and his covenant with Abraham, even more so that each of the 7.7 billion people could have a personal relationship and conversation with God through Jesus Christ.

Now I look at Moses, (Exodus 2), he first was supposed to be killed as a child, then grew up in the palace of Pharaoh, was groomed as a prince. However, he had to flee to the desert after killing a man who struck out at an Israelite. In the desert God meets him at the burning bush with a mission to take the Israelites out of Egypt (Exodus 3). Here Moses' personal relationship with God started, so much so that Moses spent time with God on the Mountain in a cloud, 40 days, and 40 nights. Incidentally this was the same time of the flood in Noah's case, I quote Exodus 24:18 (KJV)

"And Moses went into the midst of the cloud, and gat him up into the mount: and Moses was in the mount 40 days and 40 nights".

Through Moses God introduced the Law of the 1st Covenant that Christ fulfilled as previously discussed in my exposition on Jesus and prayer.

The last prophet I would like to discuss who had a significant relationship with God, is Elijah. His faith at the altar of the Baal priests, I believe stirred God's heart (1 Kings 18:20-

39) and I quote three most relevant verses from the Chapter: 1Kings 18:37-39 (KJV)

"Hear me, O LORD, hear me, that this people may know that thou art the LORD God, and that thou hast turned their heart back again. Then the fire of the LORD fell, and consumed the burnt sacrifice, and the wood, and the stones, and the dust, and licked up the water that was in the trench. And when all the people saw it, they fell on their faces: and they said, The LORD, he is the God; the LORD, he is the God".

Bearing in mind that Elijah was probably the prophet who had done the most miracles and was persecuted by Ahab and Jezebel, yet Elijah met with God in the desert whilst in hiding, God even sent ravens to feed him.

One reads about the life and works of Elijah until the end of the book of 1 Kings. The paradigm shift happens when Elijah in 2

Kings Chapter 1, denounces King Ahaziah, where he commanded fire from heaven which devoured fifty men at a time because the King was consulting a foreign god, Beelzebub about his sickness, therefore the king died as Elijah prophesied. In 2 Kings 2, Elijah starts handing over to his apprentice, Elisha, and prepares to be taken up into heaven, Elijah did not die, as did not Enoch, herein 2 Kings 2:8-11 (KJV), I quote the evidence to my comment (KJV)

"And Elijah took his mantle, and wrapped it together, and smote the waters, and they were divided hither and thither, so that they two went over on dry ground. And it came to pass, when they were gone over, that Elijah said unto Elisha, ask what I shall do for thee, before I be taken away from thee. And Elisha said, I pray thee, let a double portion of thy spirit be upon me. And he said, thou hast asked a hard thing: nevertheless, if thou see me when I am

taken from thee, it shall be so unto thee; but if not, it shall not be so. And it came to pass, as they still went on, and talked, that, behold, there appeared a chariot of fire, and horses of fire, and parted them both asunder; and Elijah went up by a whirlwind into heaven".

The reason for my exposition of the walk with God of Adam, Enoch, Noah, Moses, and Elijah, is that they were prominent in their walk with God. Taking the lead from these prominent men, who were like we are, one needs to find out what made them stand out. Therefore, defining prayer as a conversation with God, one sees that there is a better way than saying ritual prayers.

Similarly, when we converse with God, one needs to in tune with Him. Unfortunately, many people hide from prayer, just like Adam and Eve did because they are ashamed of something, or they have hidden sin and the like.

Knowing God as the Holy One, the I Am, one will not enter his presence without repentance of an unholy state of mind or being. Thus, the prayerful relationship with God is a result of a clean and clear conscience, this is enabled by the grace of God, our Father at any and every event of prayer for forgiveness, notably a way of sanctifying ourselves for the presence of God.

Now I would like to define prayer for the believer as follows: a deep, intimate conversation with God, a monolog or dialogue, inspired by the surroundings, state of mind and situations. This relates to repenting or to requesting Godly intervention, in faith, that will cause change to glorify God. Prayer includes scripture, songs of praise and worship, spiritual warfare, acclamation, praying in tongues, rebuking Satan and the prophetic, all being enriched by the gifts of the Spirit.

In short, communication with God is a mindful act, in obedience to his word, through Jesus Christ, inspired by the Holy Spirt to strengthen the relationship with God himself.

What is the best time to pray?

One finds that many people call prayer time, "quiet time" and this would be either at the beginning or end of the day, or both. Then others believe they pray at any time, others make prayer a time they prepare for and believe it should be done on sackcloth with ash, this is to prove their humility to God.

Other Christians barely say grace, and in some instances get their children to do it, this helps them tick the box that they have taught their children to pray. Yet referring to my previous exposition about having a relationship with God, time you spend with God is important whenever, wherever you are.

Back to when it is best to pray, many people can concentrate better in the evening, others better in the morning. There is no specific biblical prescript on when exactly to pray, thus it is the choice of the believer.

However, if one does not pray one loses out on specific blessings and protection, if one does a quick recital it has no meaning. Thus, the relationship with God puts one in position where, one does pray for a specific time dedicated to God, morning, evening, or both. However, knowing that Godly conversation can be done any time of day or night. I find my best time with God is around midnight when everyone is asleep.

In conclusion dedicated prayer time is obligatory, but God is outside of time and always available for true prayer and worship. I quote the Psalmist's acknowledgment of his prayer time, Psalm 5:2 – 3 (KJV)

"Hearken unto the voice of my cry, my King, and my God: for unto thee will I pray. My voice shalt thou hear in the morning, O LORD; in the morning will I direct my prayer unto thee and will look up".

How often should one pray?

Previously, I have mentioned that prayer is obligatory for spiritual wellbeing, the amount of time you utilise in prayer is equal to the spiritual power you will receive from God. Prayer is a fundamental concept of inciting the spirit and neutralising the mind. People who talk much find it easy to pray, the introvert finds it difficult to pray out in speech but finds it easy to converse with God in his/her mind.

If prayer is a monolog, and we continually ask God for things, our prayer is of value for our wants and our list is only so long. In this case, a person will only pray when they need something, big or small. Is this right?

No, it is like knocking on the neighbour's door every time you need to borrow something without being their friends. If one communicates well with one's neighbour continuously and speak about other things to him/her, they will also be there for one in a time of need. Therefore, it is no use knocking on heaven's door only when one needs something, although God hears, one may not have the same results as one would have if one had a continuous prayer relationship with God.

Making prayer a dialogue will require more time, as one needs to practice this concept, it requires one to pray and listen. Thus, dedicated time to listen cannot be given whilst doing prayer in the hustle and bustle of everyday life.

In other words, although one may pray often in the day, wherever one is, which is good, the time for dialogue prayer is when it is the individual and God alone. In this instance, praying and being quiet to listen for the voice of God, through the Word of God, the Bible, or in the mind as God opens matters. The audible voice of God is only heard by few, I personally have experienced this only a few times, yet scripture, as the inaudible truth, has given me many answers in my time of need.

In closing off the deliberation on how often we should pray, my answer is as much as possible, day or night. Dedicated time for prayer remains an important part of spiritual growth. I quote Philippians 4:6-7 (KJV)

"Be careful of nothing; but in everything by prayer and supplication with thanksgiving let your requests be made known unto God. And the peace of God, which passeth all understanding, shall keep your hearts and minds through Christ Jesus".

What may one pray for?

I would like to kick-off this discussion with Jesus' discussion on asking Matthew 7:7 (KJV) (also Luke 11:9)

"Ask, and it shall be given you; seek, and ye shall find; knock, and it shall be opened unto you".

It is of utmost importance that one first understands that prayer is all about knocking on doors of opportunity, yet it is the prayerful conversation with God that will get the door opened.

Doors will open through our prayers, however taking the second part of the scripture into account, 'seek and ye shall find', one is required to do some work. Seeking solutions may be outside of prayer, nevertheless the proposed solutions to one's problems can be tested through prayer and the Holy Spirit which lives in us.

In the event of asking, scripture, and Jesus points to asking the Father, however, understanding the way to ask, brings about a change in thought. As believers go to the Father in prayer, they speak to the father's heart. Here they are sure to find heavenly action in the solutions that will come from him, through the Son and in and around us by the Holy Spirit. Consequently, the fulfilling of our request is confirmed by my quotation of Matthew 7:8-11 (KJV)

"For everyone that asketh receiveth; and he that seeketh findeth; and to him that knocketh it shall be opened. Or what man is there of you, whom if his son ask bread, will he give him a stone? Or if he asks a fish, will he give him a serpent? If ye then, being evil, know how to give good gifts unto your children, how much more shall your Father which is in heaven give good things to them that ask him?".

The inverse is also true, if a child asks his/her father for a serpent, or a scorpion, in most cases the request will not be granted because of the danger that will be imposed on the child by his/her appeal. Therefore, it is implied that a father will not put his/her child in any danger through what he gives or grants them. This is due to the father knowing what is best for the child. Consequently, a child will be protected by the decision of the father with regards to granting a request, whether it be good or bad for the child.

With the aforementioned in mind, the child too learns what the will of their father is. Hence, they may in future not ask for something that would bring about harm, or even expect to have such a request granted. Now I proceed to Jesus' words in John 14:12-14 (KJV) and I quote

"Verily, verily, I say unto you, He that believeth on me, the works that I do shall he do also; and greater works than these shall he do, because I go unto my Father. And whatsoever ye shall ask in my name, that will I do, that the Father may be glorified in the Son. If ye shall ask any thing in my name, I will do it".

This brings me to the answer on what we may pray for and as it is encapsulated in my previous quotation, if God, Father and Son will be glorified by the request in prayer, we may ask it and God will give it. At this point I would like to add a personal matter and I refer to my late mother's words. She always said, "God always hears our prayers and will give what we ask of Him, yet not when we expect it, but with His good timing".

Herewith I close the discussion with: You may ask God for and about anything, for any solution and you may reason with God, as a child in prayer about the solutions you require. Life changing decision-making and moments require consultation with God the Father, though his Son in earnest prayer. God will never fail the individual, and the power of your prayer becomes manifest by the answers God gives through people, solutions, and his abundant providence. One must not forget that the Holy Spirit that dwells in and amongst us, together with the Angelic under God's command, has direct impact on our surroundings to change, to equip and to supply our every need. I close with a quotation from Matthew 6:8(b) (KJV)

"for your Father knoweth what things ye have need of, before ye ask him".

Can one be healed if one prays for oneself?

To pray for oneself is as logical as praying for any other person. Yet, when we look at the New Testament Church, James' letter in Chapter 5 verse 13-16 he speaks in verse 13, to affliction and proposes such a person prays so that they can be happy again, also adds that they should sing psalms to aid them in becoming joyous. In verse 14 he suggests that the sick call the elders to anoint the sick with oil in the name of Jesus.

There can be a few logical reasons why the sick should call the elders for the prayer, one may be that the pain is so unbearable that the sick person fails to pray. In another case, the sick is praying for their healing but require an extension of faith from their brothers and sisters in the Lord.

The anointing with oil is a symbolic approach and is linked to the recipe of holy oil given by Moses in Exodus. Not forgetting that the oil has a bearing on the anointing of the Holy Spirit, and the calling of God on the life of individual.

In verse 16, the author speaks to one of the more important factors of being healed, it goes with forgiving others, as in the Lord's prayer. This adds another specific dimension to the pre-requisites for healing to take place. One's sins should be forgiven by God, and by the same token, one must have forgiven all those who had done harm or wrong in any way. From a physiological point of view, forgiving others, releases a person suffering from psychosomatic disorders. Therefore, forgiveness and even self-forgiveness remains important for the healing process.

This leads to another question; can a person be healed if they do not forgive themselves for pain they have caused themselves or others?

Notably, this matter needs to be debated form two angles, remorse, and forgiveness. Whilst the remorse is part and parcel of repentance, as compared to the combination of faith and action, if one has remorse but never forgives oneself, the chances are it will cause a spiritual blockage to the healing process. The unforgiveness of oneself is as bad as not forgiving someone else.

There is a reason for my conclusion, God may have healed one's body of an ailment or injury years back, if self-forgiveness had taken place, because when God forgives, there is no further account of that specific sin or the trauma it may have caused.

However, one argues about sin and sickness, it is impossible for all sickness, disease, or trauma to be linked to sin. One must never forget that God never promised that we would never get sick, experience traumatic events or financial problems if a person chooses to serve Him. I purport that neither sin, nor unforgiveness will always be the reason for not being well or contracting a disease. Herewith, I quote Job 2:1-8, where God allowed Job to be tested through the works of Satan, in the end it was for Job's good although he went through much body, physiological and psychological pain. Tests, in different categories, mould and make us so that we can serve others better. To this end I conclude that if one has not experienced pain, sickness, or traumatic events, one will not be able to serve or help someone going through the same. Our experiences make us feel with those who require healing or solutions.

Now to the Question, can one pray for personal healing? Oh yes, without a doubt, God meets the intention of the individual's heart. I have prayed for myself about personal health issues and God has healed me, yet in other cases God has reduced pain in my body and has allowed the healing process to take place naturally. Most certainly, God hears the prayer of his children and the faith we have, and His will, are key to healing and the answered prayer. Remember the best one to pray and discuss personal problems with, is God.

Mediators and intercessors help but they often do not have all it takes to discuss the need for healing with God. Yet all prayer, and communal prayer, brings results as promised in God's word.

What about success and prosperity in prayer?

Throughout my journey with Jesus, from the time I was baptized as a believer (July 1975) I can list the success that God had brought upon my life through prayer. Probably if I had known how God could orchestrate success a younger age, I may have been much more successful.

My parents taught me about asking God for that which was required, and they did this well. At home as a child, we were taught to fast and pray, yet at the same time I knew my parents fasted even to ensure that there was food on the table for their six children. My dad had left his job to become a full-time pastor in 1977 and in faith he started a congregation in the town named Vryheid in KwaZulu Natal, South Africa. This was a small farming town, about 30 000 residents at that time.

My dad had acquired land and got me involved in drawing the Church plans, my first church project as a teenager of about 16. I was taught that success comes from learning to do things for yourself, and that no one can take away experience from you. Two things my dad taught me well while I was at school, one was how to do electrical work, for example, my father allowed me to work with him as his apprentice from a very early age, although I never qualified as an electrician. Secondly, he taught me how to read and draw building plans and how to lay bricks, and I also never qualified to do such, I matriculated at the age of 17 and was ready to become an architect. Because I had no specific knowledge about university and because I parents could not afford to send us to university I was like other boys, ready to go to the army to do national service.

I then joined the South African Air Force to work as an apprentice on Mirage fighter Aircraft. This was far from my dream; however, it was a good start to my journey through life, I had a means of earning money although I shelved my dream of becoming and architect. Yet, if I had known it was not wrong to pray for funds to go to university, and if I had knowledge about the academia, I could probably have had a different start to life.

Why did I start with this life story? Because there are many young people today who could start off on life's journey to become what they want to be. Kocher, (2019) comes up with a rather simple secular formula for success namely: DREAMS + VISION + GOALS + ACTIONS = SUCCESS. Although his formula works, one could have more success by not leaving out knowledge, faith and prayer. This triad enables the actions to be much more successful. Accordingly, I propose a spiritual variant of a formula for success namely of a formula for success is a simple one namely: S success = (D dreams + V vison + G goals) * (K knowledge + F faith) * (A action + P prayer). My proposed formula is very Biblical, as Paul writes action without faith is death, and Jesus says faith can move mountains, both these sayings are incorporated into my formula.

Similarly, the saying, knowledge is power cannot be negated, conversely, if I had the knowledge about the academia, I have today, I would have approached life much differently. Do I regret the success I attained through traveling down the path I did? No certainly not, it still led me to success, yet I thought prayer and faith would do it all as I was taught.

I missed two fundamental factors for success, knowledge and in many cases action, through procrastinating and not grabbing hold of each opportunity that came my way. The way to success is not by luck, it comes as a journey and can be measured in so many ways. This journey incorporates the gifts of the spirit in 1 Corinthians 12:7-11. Mastering these gifts brings about the ability to be spiritually and carnally successful, and I refer to three of the nine gifts namely: knowledge, wisdom, and discernment.

These are required especially when one takes up a leadership role. All said, I do believe that God has intended that each of us become successful in what we do. However, to become successful in prayer, and for success in life, one must climb and move mountains, endure hardship, bring about and cause change, make mistakes, forgive and forget and in some cases act on impulse.

Back to the question, may I pray for success? Most certainly but success is not only prayer, it is part and parcel of a formula.

I believe God will allow us to live out our dreams and even so He may even add vision that needs to be engulfed by faith and knowledge of the matter. Just as faith cannot stand alone without action, so too one will need to put in enough prayer to make the triad work toward personal success. Prayer with determination, faith and vision unlocks doors, and moves mountains the eye cannot see.

May I include animals in my prayer?

I will never forget when I was about 16 years old, my parents were away at a conference and my dog had a bad injury. For me this was extremely bad, although the vet had stitched him up, the wound became infectious. I did not have the knowledge to nurse a dog, but I knew how to pray, and I did put prayer into action for my dog, and he did recover. Notably, I was at an age where I had learned to pray about matters, I did not debate it theologically, and it worked.

The question is, can we pray for our animals? Yes, I believe so, not that they are offered eternal life, as humans with salvation. Yet, God hears the prayer of the righteous, for their good. Therefore, the believer's possessions, animals and artefacts can carry the blessing of God.

Summary

In this chapter, I have discussed, at length what prayer is, explaining what the best time and how often one should pray. I touched on the vast amount of matters a believer can pray about and for, and how one prays for and about oneself. This chapter also discussed healing, forgiveness, and the results of unforgiveness. It closed with prayer for success and prosperity and lastly the blessing of God also reaching our, possessions, pets, or animals. In closing this Chapter, one should be able to table a prayer worksheet.

Personal Prayer Worksheet

This worksheet can be used to interpret prayer topics and to plan for action, use your interpretation to plan a prayer routine.

1. Prayer topic My interpretation and action

2. What prayer means to me

3. My best time for prayer

4. How I should pray

5. What I should pray for

6. Praying for my healing and other's

7. Praying for blessing, success, and prosperity

8. Praying blessing and protection upon possessions and pets

CHAPTER 3

Jesus and Prayer

To answer the question on Jesus and prayer, I propose a journey through the gospels, Matthew, Mark, Luke, and John ending with the delivery of the Holy Spirit promise in Acts. The objective of this journey is to find out why prayer was so important to Jesus, and how prayer was a primary source of His spiritual power. Here I will incorporate Karl Barth's premise that Jesus, when he lived on earth was fully human, yet fully God.

Notably, these two aspects, God, and Human, in one being have concerned many theologians and church fathers throughout the about 2000 year's existence of Christianity. Why I feel comfortable with the two aspects in one, is that Jesus being the only begotten Son of God (John 3:16) brings meaning to the humanness and the godliness of Christ into one dispensation, the life of Christ. However, it is rather difficult to imagine God fully humanised in the growth of Jesus from fetus to where he died on the cross of Calvary to earn our eternal salvation.

Then God, in the human Jesus, was manifest even in his temple teaching as a child (Matthew, Mark, Luke). Speaking to Isaiah in the temple, his godly purpose was first introduced to the Sanhedrin, but being spiritually blind they could not recognise the Messiah who was standing in front of them.

Jesus being the Son of God, was conversing in his mind with the Father and the Holy Spirit and had the full knowledge of the Word, because it was him (John 1:1). Thus, by implication, biblical knowledge influences the relationship between God and man. This links the studying of the Bible to prayer for reinforcement of what God said, and to remind us of His promises. Furthermore, this prompts us to recall foundational truths while we pray or when we are tempted as Jesus was (Matthew 4:1 – 11; Mark 1:12-13).

Jesus' Fasting and Prayer

Matthew 4 starts with Jesus' 40 day fast in the desert: the Bible tells us that he ate nothing for this entire period. It amazes me that the Son of God fasts for a full 40 days, privately, before his ministry begins. It almost seems as if there is a break between his life and his ministry as he prepares spiritually for the final journey of his divine visit to earth. Similarly, Moses spent 40 Days on the Mountain with God before he was entrusted with the law, temple, and the ark of the covenant: he too fasted 40 days and nights in the desert. Surprisingly, Jesus says he came to fulfil the law that was shared with Moses on the Mount (Exodus 24:14-18; chapters 25-31). In this time God shared so much with Moses, Genesis, the temple plans, and the law, almost as if it were a heavenly induction.

Likewise, the Son of God, Jesus, moves to the desert, for 40 Days. At this time he was the only one who had the masterplan of the Father for salvation, Jesus, and the Father share, for 40 days, his mission, the fulfilment of prophecy, of which Satan had to be left out completely. This the 40 days of fasting encompassed Christ's mission of fulfilment, yet Satan visits Jesus to overthrow an eternal mission. It is as if Satan repeats the first Adamic visit with tempting words, so it is no wonder the Biblical writers refer to the first and second Adam.

I attempt to expose a lesson about mission fasting, firstly, Satan will always attempt to overthrow God's work before a big change is eminent. Secondly, Adam and Eve, and eternal friendship between God and Man, derailed by temptation. Secondly, whilst Moses was on Mt Sanai, Satan works with the Israelites to build a golden calf. Lastly, after Jesus and the Father are in union through a 40 day fast, Satan visits Jesus, attempting to derail God's mission. To this end, the Son of God speaks back to every scripture used by Satan, as he attempts to overthrow the mission of Christ.

Thus, to those men and women of God, who fast about a God given mission, remember, Satan will try his best to turn your heart away from what God has ordained you to do. He will not tempt you on what you are good at, he will try to use your weakest structure or ability to make you fall or change direction. Be wary of him, do not fear failure, comply with the mission blueprint and, I repeat, be faithful to what God called you for.

For Jesus' opinion on the practice of fasting I quote directly from the King James version; Matthew 6:16-17 (KJV),

"Moreover when ye fast, be not, as the hypocrites, of a sad countenance: for they disfigure their faces, that they may appear unto men to fast. Verily I say unto you, they have their reward. But thou, when thou fastest, anoint thine head, and wash thy face; that thou appear not unto men to fast, but unto thy Father which is in secret: and thy Father, which seeth in secret, shall reward thee openly".

Fasting brings about unexplained power, I have experienced first-hand intervention from God, when it is done in humility and when seeking his face. I recall many moments where I had to have change in the corporate space, even when we prayed for thousands or millions of Rand for projects, God provided this immediately or through a process. Thus, the fasting phenomenon can be broken down into three layers namely: spiritual, need and impact.

One should first get around the spiritual side of fasting, this is a humbling experience where Jesus speaks to his disciples about the demonic in Mathew 17:21 and Mark 9:29. Here Jesus speaks to the disciples about removing the demonic from a person, this is spiritual, and denotes that some demons will cling on if the person driving them out is not spiritually capable of removing them.

It is implied by Jesus, that people who fast and pray have a loaded spiritual battery that can move the mountains. This does add a spiritual dimension to the works of faith.

Addressing the need through fasting does not come through the sympathy a person gets from bystanders because of the abstaining from food or drink, it is about the purpose of the fast in the spiritual realm that counts.

When needs are addressed in the spiritual realm one may not see how God changes or rearranges life, moments, people and or resources in a moment. The moments of addressing needs are realised through the spiritual and bodily humility, a kind of spiritual sacrifice that addresses a need or needs through fasting and prayer. However, a spiritual need brings the Holy Spirit into the situation, and when the Pneuma[i] of God is part of the equation the situation is in God's control. It is no wonder God's words come through the prophet Isaiah (57:15) (KJV)

"For thus saith the high and lofty One that inhabiteth eternity, whose name is Holy; I dwell in the high and holy place, with him

also that is of a contrite and humble spirit, to revive the spirit of the humble, and to revive the heart of the contrite ones".

The level of impact after fasting is dependent on the humility, the need, and the acts of God though the Holy Spirit and the Angelic, to make impactful change on a situation. These changes may vary from miraculous healing, to providence or even a great wave of Godly movement though towns and cities, commonly termed revival.

Jesus' ministry on earth moved thousands of hearts, changed lives, brought wisdom into situations, and healed the sick. Thus again, by implication, Jesus' ministry was a foundation for the exposition of the power of the believer through the fundamentals of prayer and fasting.

Prayer and the disciples

Just after Jesus' ministry started, he delivers the sermon on the mount, his disciples are with him and the multitudes. Jesus starts off in Matthew 6:5 by teaching his followers and disciples not to make up prayers for an audience. Jesus condemns prayers that are done in high places, churches, synagogues that are a repetition of words or recitals. These prayers, he said, relate to hypocrisy and have no spiritual meaning and may not be answered.

So why did Jesus start off by condemning ritual prayers? He was setting the scene, because ritual prayer was an order, people prayed out loud for all to hear, repeated words and sentences over and over, expecting heavenly favour. I have experienced this in many walks of life, in prayer meetings, in churches where the louder you pray the more powerful the prayer seems to be. So, is praying out loud wrong? Certainly not but praying to impress others will not bring much success. When we pray, the answer to the prayer is rooted in the sincerity of our heart and mind. Jesus said the same about fasting which I dealt with previously.

In Matthew 6:6 (GNB), *Jesus leaves his audience with a key to have prayer answered,*

"But when you pray, go to your room, close the door, and pray to your Father, who is unseen. And your Father, who sees what you do in private, will reward you".

Yet, this may add confusion, does this statement annul public prayer, certainly not, because Jesus also says in Matthew 18:20 (GNB);

"if two or three are gathered in my name, I am in their midst".

But his does however bring us to the point where Jesus differentiates between gather to glorify God, to pray and being in relationship with the Son in private prayer.

In this respect, I have seen many Christians depend on intercessors to pray for them, this is good, but is it not better to pray and have a prayer bond with the Saviour in person?

No offence to intercessors, but we need Christians, believers, to pray for themselves in private and to believe that the father will answer their prayers through their own faith. This will empower the entire church of God to do the works of faith. This leads me to the next key Jesus leaves to answered prayer.

Matthew 6:8 (b) (GNB) relates to the Jesus' Father in heaven, knowing us personally through prayer and I quote:

"Your Father already knows what you need before you ask him".

I remember when my children used to want something, they would hint and not ask. Yet I knew exactly what they wanted or what they were hinting about, because I was an integral part of their life. My answer would be, why do you hint? Just ask and I can discuss your need or want with you. This Jesus builds in before he starts speaking to the model prayer, the "Our Father" as we know it.

As Jesus continues to teach, he builds a model prayer into his already packed sermon. Yet, this prayer, even though to many, has become a recital and or ritual, has endless value in the principles of prayer. Therefore, without hesitance, it becomes vital to unpack Matthew 6:9-13 in a way that can be useful in personal prayer.

Jesus had prayer sessions with his disciples in his entire ministry, the last at Gethsemane as recorded well in John 17 when Jesus prays the high priestly prayer. This prayer we will also unpack after understanding the building blocks of the Lord's prayer. I will use the King James version to accommodate traditional thinking although I do believe simpler English could be more appropriate in personal prayer. So, doing, it would be best to first build on traditional English then I will switch to the Good News Bible.

Matthew 6:9-13(KJV)

"After this manner therefore pray ye: Our Father which art in heaven, hallowed be thy name. Thy kingdom come. Thy will be done in earth, as it is in heaven. Give us this day our daily bread. And forgive us our debts, as we forgive our debtors. And lead us not into temptation but deliver us from evil: For thine is the kingdom, and the power, and the glory, forever, Amen".

I have found that many Christians switch from universal to high English when they pray, this may be due to the use of the King James Version of the Bible. This phenomenon probably reiterates respect for the Godhead in prayer, nothing wrong with this. The prayer, as I have mentioned, has fourteen building blocks namely:

1. Our Father
2. Hallowed be thy name
3. Thy Kingdom
4. Thy will
5. Earth and heaven
6. Provision of daily bread
7. Personal forgiveness
8. Us forgiving others
9. Protection from temptation
10. Delivering us from evil influence
11. Confirmation of God's kingdom
12. Confirmation of God's power
13. Confirmation of God's Glory
14. Confirmation of eternity

This prayer as identified, is jam packed with the richness of 14 Christian values that extend beyond our conscious and sub-conscious minds. These are spiritual emblems that can only be fully appreciated when using each of them to pray and increase the vocabulary and meaning through practice. Prayer is the most powerful tool that has been left for the church by Jesus himself. To do minor justice to the capability of the model prayer. The process of unpacking the fourteen principles of the Lord's prayer follows.

Our Father

First and foremost, Jesus says there is only one way to the Father and that is through himself, I quote John 14:6 (KJV):

"Jesus saith unto him, I am the way, the truth, and the life: no man cometh unto the Father, but by me".

However, the Godhead, three in one, Father, Son and Holy Spirit needs to be outlined when contemplating the term heavenly Father. One should never get confused with other religions who also proclaim a trinity. There are not many ways to the Father as is universally proclaimed. It is important to note that our father is Jehovah, and the only way he has become the Father of Gentiles, was by the sacrifice of his Son, Jesus Christ. In addition to my previous comments, it should be noted that when Jesus gave the disciples the model prayer, it was for the Jewish nation, he had not yet died for the redemption of sin. Therefore, the Spirit of God was on Jesus at this time, it was not yet sent to dwell in and among the Church.

Thus Jesus, fully man and fully God currently, reveals his Father as the first and foremost aspect of prayer. In the same vein, Jesus identifies the place from where God reigns, heaven. Unfortunately, we know very little about heaven except for the descriptions Jesus gave in parables, some aspects highlighted in the books of the apocrypha and the biblical revelation of John. The best example of prayer and heaven is the throne room as revealed, I quote Revelation 5:8 (KJV) about the prayers of the saints;

"And when he had taken the book, the four beasts and four and twenty elders fell down before the Lamb, having every one of them harps, and golden vials full of odours, which are the prayers of saints. Other translations speak to the prayers of the saints as being as incense before God".

Leading back to the concept of "Father" Jesus brings perspective by equating the fathers who do evil, yet look after their children, with the heavenly Father who knows no sin (Luke 11:11-13). This brings us to the aspects of fatherly love, the knowledge of a father about the child, its needs, wants and urgencies. The aspects of prayer in relation to the Father is a direct family relationship with God, through Jesus Christ.

In respect of prayer, we address God the Father through Jesus Christ who has saved us from our sinful nature. Through the saving grace we have access to the Father who cares for us and who oversees the entire universe.

Hallowed be thy name

Going back to the Greek word where "Hallowed" originated from ἁγιάζω, hagiazō phonetically pronounced hag-ee-ad'-zo from (Strongs: G40); to make holy, that is, (ceremonially) purify or consecrate; (mentally) to venerate: - hallow, be holy, sanctify". In the latter, the word hallow speaks to the holiness of God, in other words, Holy is God's name. In this ultra-holy state of God, his holiness is proclaimed throughout the Bible. Referring to God's holiness one looks back at Moses' meeting with God at the burning bush in the desert Exodus 3:4-5 (KJV)

"And when the LORD saw that he turned aside to see, God called unto him out of the midst of the bush, and said, Moses, Moses. And he said, here am I". And he said, draw not nigh hither: put off thy shoes from off thy feet, for the place whereon thou standest is holy ground".

When we encounter God face to face, we realise His holiness first, this is unlike our state of mortality. Even though we try to be holy, the human nature falls short of the holiness which is of God. Yet, through our salvation experience we become holy, or sinless, by grace. By implication, our human nature needs to be subdued by notion of acceptance of who we have become in

Christ. Not to boast of holiness, as some Christians do, but to be sanctified by God through the Holy Spirit, living in the flesh but controlled by the Spirit of God.

Conversely, looking at sanctification in the Old Testament: God called Moses and the prophets to do this with Israel, the people of God had to cleanse themselves before presenting themselves to God, especially so in Exodus and Leviticus.

Jesus prays for his disciples and the coming church in John 17:17 and 19

"*Sanctify them through thy truth: thy word is truth. And for their sakes I sanctify myself, that they also might be sanctified through the truth*".

Jesus is preparing for his final hour; in this he calls for the sanctification of his then and coming disciples because he knew it is expected by the Father. Thus, I conclude that holiness is part and parcel of the Christian package and as Paul writes to the Ephesians, I quote 1:3-4

"*Blessed be the God and Father of our Lord Jesus Christ, who hath blessed us with all spiritual blessings in heavenly places in Christ: According as he hath chosen us in him before the foundation of the world, that we should be holy and without blame before him in love*".

Therefore, proclaiming God's holiness in prayer, brings about the notion that we need to pray and clear our conscience of that which would defile the holiness of God. Our Father needs to be approached in Christ, through whom the Grace of God has been made manifest in His holiness by cleansing us from any wrongdoing.

Thy Kingdom

Jesus, at the start of his ministry in Matthew 4:17(b) (KJV) proclaims the new kingdom that comes

"Repent: for the kingdom of heaven is at hand".

Then in Matthew 6:10 Jesus adds the same to his prayer, this is in direct relation to the kingdom which the disciples were called into. It is implied that the kingdom Jesus proclaims is that of the born again. Matthew 4:23 Jesus relates to the gospel of the kingdom, a kingdom not ruled by men but by Jesus himself. Then in the prayer Jesus speaks to this Kingdom as the Father's Kingdom, bringing about a new dimension to the spiritual populace, the kingdom of believers.

Two rules to be obeyed when joining the kingdom of God one in John 3:3 "*Jesus answered and said unto him, Verily, verily, I say unto thee, except a man be born again, he cannot see the kingdom of God"*. The second, based on Matthew 4:17 where repentance is key.

The construct of God's kingdom is different, it is not a carnal kingdom, although it houses mortal beings such as you and me. Jesus speaks to Pilate before his crucifixion wherein, he explains his Kingdom in John 18:36 (b) (KJV)

"My kingdom is not of this world: if my kingdom were of this world, then would my servants fight, that I should not be delivered to the Jews: but now is my kingdom not from hence".

This infers that the Kingdom of Jesus is a heavenly one and is not subject to earthly rules but spiritual ones. It is made up of born-again believers who have their names written in the Lamb's book of life.

Will there be exclusions from the kingdom? It seems so according to Matthew 7:21-23 (KJV)

"Not everyone that saith unto me, Lord, Lord, shall enter into the kingdom of heaven; but he that doeth the will of my Father which is in heaven. Many will say to me in that day, Lord, Lord, have we not prophesied in thy name? and in thy name have cast out devils? and in thy name done many wonderful works? And then will I profess unto them, I never knew you: depart from me, ye that work iniquity".

One should not fear entering the kingdom, yet not making it, relates to spiritual failure and probably pride and complacency. Thus prayer, sanctification, and supplication, will reduce the chances of not making it to heaven where the kingdom is.

God's will

Have you ever asked yourself the question, "what is the will of God about my life?" and possibly, "how does God see my future?" or even "does God really care about me and my situations?". I will attempt to take up the questions in the discussion about the will of God, yet it is my objective to get you to start experiencing the will of God in your life. Jesus speaks of himself conforming to the will of God in John 5:30 (KJV)

"I can of mine own self do nothing: as I hear, I judge and my judgment is just; because I seek not mine own will, but the will of the Father which hath sent me".

Imagine Jesus, knowing the will of God to such an extent that he knew of his crucifixion as a sacrifice for our sin. In his mind he had to grapple with the human elements of the supreme mission that he had to accomplish. God's greater plan he understood well, yet he himself had to go through every step of his ministry, the last supper, Gethsemane, judgement and the cross. However, he still says, "Father not my will, but yours be done".

Back to our own world, in my opinion, only God has the bigger picture about our lives, yet we so often try to do our own thing.

How many of us do career planning with God? How many of us do family planning with God? How many plan or day with him?

I know there are many Pastors and Christians who condemn asking God for signs that indicate his will, my question is, is it wrong to seek Godly direction? It should be a principle to ask God what he thinks first. No wonder the Holy Spirit was sent to dwell in and amongst us, else this guidance would not be applicable. In fact, any big changes or decisions I make, I consult God in prayer so that I can be guided to success and not failure. I reiterate, God knows the consequences of our decisions better than we do and for a specific reason, we know the past, we may to some extent understand the here and now, but God knows the future.

This leads me to the question I asked earlier, "Does God really care about me and my situation?". The direct answer is, he most definitely does.

However, we cannot blame God for the wrong decisions we made, opportunities we let go of, consequences of our sin, things others have done to us. The good thing about God is his grace always allows for repair of things we have done outside of his will. God will not divorce his family, yet to be part of a family calls for house rules, example "in our house we don't shout at each other" and family discipline, "we wash and clean up before going to bed".

God's will, however, would relate to the bigger picture, a wider responsibility of the individual and his/her family and their management of their spiritual life in general. I quote the words of Jesus in Matthew 12:50 (KJV)

"For whosoever shall do the will of my Father which is in heaven, the same is my brother, and sister, and mother". Let us walk and talk the will of God through our consultation and conversation with God in prayer.

Earth and heaven

There is a fundamental difference between heaven and earth, it is almost as if heaven is a picturesque place where nothing is out of place and where nothing can go wrong. The perfect place where God rules without any human interference, and this is so. God is in command of the entire universe, the Angelic, the demonic and humankind.

Unfortunately, we know too little about heaven, heavenly places, and heavenly beings, all we know is written in the Bible, minor accounts of heavenly visitations and the like. But what I can confirm that as real as what the planet earth is, heaven also exists. One should bear in mind that the universe is controlled by God from his throne, with Jesus on his right hand, we are subjected to heavenly intervention through our prayers and manifestations. Jesus confirms this in Matthew 18:18 -19 (KJV)

"Verily I say unto you, Whatsoever ye shall bind on earth shall be bound in heaven: and whatsoever ye shall loose on earth shall be loosed in heaven. Again, I say unto you, that if two of you shall agree on earth as touching anything that they shall ask, it shall be done for them of my Father which is in heaven".

With this scripture in mind, I say that Christians are not using their authority on earth or in heaven for several reasons. One, they do not know what the scripture says. Two, they do not agree together in prayer, and their faith falters at the sight of the problem or situation. Three, they have never experienced the power of the authoritative acts of the Church.

One should never underestimate the powers of the heavenlies, whether by the Holy Spirit or the Angelic. When God intervenes, the outcomes are far above science and human deliberation. Similarly, one finds that prayer is the key to heavenly intervention on earth.

Provision of daily bread

Have you ever wondered why the Lord's prayer asks only for the day's provision? It seems to contravene millennial thinking, where all is about instant gratification, insurance, saving for the future, not having enough, wealth creation and the like. But there is reason for this contradiction as Jesus releases us from a future burden though prayer, it is about the provision for the here and now, because that counts most.

Taking a closer look at scripture about providence I quote Matthew 6:25-26 (KJV)

"Therefore I say unto you, take no thought for your life, what ye shall eat, or what ye shall drink; nor yet for your body, what ye shall put on. Is not the life more than meat, and the body than raiment? Behold the fowls of the air: for they sow not, neither do they reap, nor gather into barns; yet your heavenly Father feedeth them. Are ye not much better than they? ".

Thus, it seems, that in prayer it is of more importance to concentrate on what is required for the moment and the day than to worry and be concerned about the matters of tomorrow.

Moreover, Jesus speaks to the cares of tomorrow in Matthew 6:31 – 34 (KJV)

"Therefore take no thought, saying, what shall we eat? or, what shall we drink? or, wherewithal shall we be clothed? (For after all these things do the Gentiles seek: for your heavenly Father knoweth that ye have need of all these things. But seek ye first the kingdom of God, and his righteousness; and all these things shall be added unto you. Take therefore no thought for the morrow: for the morrow shall take thought for the things of itself. Sufficient unto the day is the evil thereof".

Therefore, the key to success is, first and foremost seeking and living in the kingdom of God, and then it seems from scripture the providence of God, for the future will be added to the life of the believer. In conclusion then, God will provide for today and tomorrow, we pray for the provision of the moment.

Personal forgiveness

Since Genesis, the days of Adam and Eve, God has been in the forgiveness business, and I am sure every sin of man has come before Him. The book Isaiah written as late as about 539 BC, relates to the sin of the people, I quote from verse 59:12-13 (KJV)

"For our transgressions are multiplied before thee, and our sins testify against us: for our transgressions are with us; and as for our iniquities, we know them; In transgressing and lying against the LORD, and departing away from our God, speaking oppression and revolt, conceiving and uttering from the heart words of falsehood".

Even worse, Jesus bore the sins of humankind on the cross of Calvary so that we may have forgiveness and that we can be part of God's kingdom. Yet personal forgiveness is something much deeper than regret or the labouring of the conscious mind. Key to forgiveness is repentance, without saying sorry or showing remorse for a wrongdoing, forgiveness would not be possible. Yet it has been a practice in Churches, to get people to pay penance in numerous ways to earn forgiveness. This practice is wrong, and I purport that forgiveness cannot be earned or paid for in any other way but through repentance in prayer through Jesus Christ our advocate and mediator. To be forgiven is simple and explicit, repent before God, revert from the sin, stop doing wrong and be forgiven by God's grace.

Hebrews 1:2–3 (KJV) lines up well with the discussion on the Father's forgiveness,

"Hath in these last days spoken unto us by his Son, whom he hath appointed heir of all things, by whom also he made the worlds; Who being the brightness of his glory, and the express image of his person, and upholding all things by the word of his power, when he had by himself purged our sins, sat down on the right hand of the Majesty on high".

Whilst Jesus is at the right hand of the father to ensure forgiveness of sins, this confirms forgiveness according to Mica 7:19 (KJV)

"He will turn again, he will have compassion upon us; he will subdue our iniquities; and thou wilt cast all their sins into the depths of the sea".

One concludes that God does not just forgive, he also forgets the sin. This leaves us with another question, if God has forgiven us our sins, why can't we forgive ourselves for the sin? It seems to be a human inclination to accept forgiveness in terms of the size or severity of the sin.

In some cases, the consequence of the sin remains and become the reminder of what we did wrong.

Therefore, the more accurate way to ensure forgiveness is to work through the consequences without returning to the sin or committing the same errors again. The key is that God forgives, and forgiveness is justified by a quotation from 1 John 1:9 (KJV)

"If we confess our sins, he is faithful and just to forgive us our sins, and to cleanse us from all unrighteousness".

Forgiving others

On being forgiven Jesus places an exclusion on personal forgiveness. Mark 11:25-26 (KJV)

"And when ye stand praying, forgive, if ye have fought against any: that your Father also which is in heaven may forgive you your trespasses. But if ye do not forgive, neither will your Father which is in heaven forgive your trespasses".

It is quite clear that forgiveness only has one price tag for the individual, to be forgiven you must forgive. Yet, it often happens that people do the same thing over and over and it gets to a point where one cannot forgive any longer. In this case Jesus also answered his disciples, and here I refer to Luke 17:3-4 (KJV)

"Take heed to yourselves: If thy brother trespass against thee, rebuke him; and if he

repents, forgive him. And if he trespasses against thee seven times in a day, and seven times in a day turn again to thee, saying, I repent; thou shalt forgive him".

Again, the repentance of the person in question becomes important. Here a question arises, what if a person does not repent? Then we can take the paradigm of Jesus when those who crucified Him, were casting lots on his clothing, Luke 23:34 (KJV)

"*Then said Jesus, Father, forgive them; for they know not what they do. And they parted his raiment and cast lots*".

This implies we should forgive even those who have done us dishonour even though they have not repented. The crux of the matter is, if you need forgiveness, you must forgive.

Protection from temptation

Temptation started way back with Adam and Eve in Genesis 3, and unfortunately Satan or Lucifer and his demonic have never stopped trying to move humankind to disobey God and his ordinances. Temptation leads to sin, yet it is not yet sin until an individual has succumbed to act out the inducement.

One needs to understand that sin comes from a physiological need to practice or do something extraordinary that may bring harm to the spirit, mind, or body of an individual, or a multiple of individuals. This is usually, as was in the garden of Eden, an act of disobedience or unfaithfulness to God, God's will, another person or even in some cases the laws of nature.

To understand why we need to be protected from temptation is simple, because even Jesus, the Son of God was tempted. The problem with temptation is that the enticement will probably appeal to the psyche of an individual in one way or another. This appeal comes through sight, hearing, touch, taste, or smell. It appeals to our senses, speaks to the conscious and subconscious mind, and may be thought over until it is acted or not acted upon. Temptation can be an immediate interaction, or it can happen over time, and in many instances has devastating consequences. Unfortunately, temptation is an ingestion of a probable sin.

It is no wonder the Lord's prayer speaks to guarding us from temptation, and in this case prayer and continuous prayer protects the individual from sin and its aftermaths.

In this case I would refer to Paul's first letter to the Corinthians where he says in 10:12-13 (KJV)

"Wherefore let him that thinketh he standeth take heed lest he fall. There hath no temptation taken you, but such as is common to man: but God is faithful, who will not suffer you to be tempted above that ye are able; but will with the temptation also make a way to escape, that ye may be able to bear it".

Therefore, it is also a fact that in temptation God could allow for the outcome without an individual failing.

As a Christian you will not be free of temptation, but you can overcome each of them by the spiritual protection that God offers through the Holy Spirit and the cleansing blood of Christ. On temptation I conclude with James 1:12 (KJV)

"Blessed is the man that endureth temptation: for when he is tried, he shall receive the crown of life, which the Lord hath promised to them that love him".

Delivering us from evil

The spiritual realm is both congested with good (the Angelic) and evil (the demonic). Then the most important we have in the spiritual realm is the Holy Spirit, third person of the Godhead or trinity.

The construct of the spiritual world allows for battles between the Angelic and demonic, the battlefield only accessible to us though prayer and intercession.

Paul writes to the Ephesians and cohorts the church to live in the spirit and to understand that the battle of prayer is greater than what can be seen with the naked eye. I quote Ephesians 6:12 (KJV)

"For we wrestle not against flesh and blood, but against principalities, against powers, against the rulers of the darkness of this world, against spiritual wickedness in high places".

One must understand that wickedness and evil can be instigated through the spirit into those who do not follow Christ. This evil can be in the form of different spirts of evil, murderous, lying, corrupt, adulterous and the like. From these we need to be protected, not only in person but families, communities, churches, companies, large organisations, countries and even continents.

One must remember, Satan is the deceiver, fraudster, liar, and master of evil. To this end, our protection in the spiritual realm must be against his plans and traps. Firstly, this links into temptation, and secondly his evil works are carried out by humanity. Lastly, he thrives on the fall of the believer, whether it be through trial or temptation. Here is the good news, Isaiah 54:17 (KJV) reads:

"No weapon that is formed against thee shall prosper; and every tongue that shall rise against thee in judgment thou shalt

condemn. This is *the heritage of the servants of the LORD, and their righteousness* is *of me, saith the LORD".*

I profess that we should never hunt down Satan, give him credit for his evil or even spend time discussing him. The Glory of God surpasses and conquers all evil. We are the sons and daughters of God, and in that vein, we should not fear evil but be prepared to conquer it by the blood of the Lamb.

Confirmation of God's kingdom

The kingdom of God was first recorded officially by Jesus in the Gospels, Matthew, Mark, Luke, and John. It is also recorded that Christ reigns over the kingdom of God, and that it is the true Church of Jesus Christ. Therefore, a believer should remember that, although the earth has many kingdoms, we are sure of one kingdom of Christ, consisting of many nations. I believe this Kingdom has been around since the resurrection of Christ and will live on through the thousand years of peace where Jesus will reign over the world in person as Messiah and as God's Son.

What we do in prayer is to confirm that we are part of God's greater kingdom, this means we would have to pray for many other people outside of our family, church, or direct community. Remember the Great Commission as recorded in Matthew 28:19-20 (KJV)

"Go ye therefore, and teach all nations, baptizing them in the name of the Father, and of the Son, and of the Holy Ghost: Teaching them to observe all things whatsoever I have commanded you: and, lo, I am with you always, even unto the end of the world. Amen".

This commission of making disciples increases the Kingdom of God, both on earth and in heaven. The increase of the kingdom is always twofold, each person that accepts Christ as his/her saviour enters the Kingdom on earth and inherits eternal life in the Kingdom of heaven. In other words, pilgrims on earth on their way to a destination as citizens of heaven.

Confirmation of God's power

Jesus starts off the conversation about the great commission with his disciples, of course excluding Judas, in Matthew 28:18 (KJV) and I quote

"And Jesus came and spake unto them, saying, all power is given unto me in heaven and in earth".

This confirmation of authority to Jesus the Son of God is confirmed and it brings the same authority through the Holy Spirit upon the Church, or Kingdom of Christ. In this instance we need to look much further into the power that was invested in the Church on the promise Jesus gives about the Holy Spirit. Jesus, just before the ascension into heaven says his last words to the disciples on the mount of Olives, Acts 1:8 (KJV)

"But ye shall receive power, after that the Holy Ghost is come upon you: and ye shall be witnesses unto me both in Jerusalem, and in all Judaea, and in Samaria, and unto the uttermost part of the earth".

I maintain that the exposed power of prayer and fasting is evident as we follow the preparation period of ten days before Pentecost.

One should never underestimate the potential that is released through preparing oneself spiritually and faithfully to achieve the intended outcome. In this case the disciples were sent to wait in Jerusalem until they received the power of the Spirit which was promised.

I relate the previous exposition to Acts 2:1-4 (KJV)

"And when the day of Pentecost was fully come, they were all with one accord in one place. And suddenly there came a sound from heaven as of a rushing mighty wind, and it filled all the house where they were sitting. And there appeared unto them cloven tongues like as of fire, and it sat upon each of them. And they were all filled with the Holy Ghost, and began to speak with other tongues, as the Spirit gave them utterance".

The related piece of scripture gives real evidence of the power of God descending on the believers in about AD 33, the birth of the kingdom Church of Christ. Jesus says to his disciples in Luke 9:27(KJV)

"But I tell you of a truth, there be some standing here, which shall not taste of death, till they see the kingdom of God".

I allege that the Kingdom was born on the day of Pentecost and the words of Jesus in the aforesaid verse had come into fulfilment, the disciples did see the birth of the kingdom before they saw death, yet Judas was excluded, he died before the kingdom was born through the power of the Holy Spirit.

And in conclusion John the Baptist foretold the baptism with fire in Matthew 3:11 (KJV)

"I indeed baptize you with water unto repentance: but he that cometh after me is mightier than I, whose shoes I am not worthy to bear he shall baptize you with the Holy Ghost, and with fire".

Confirmation of God's Glory

In Gethsemane Jesus affirms the Glory of God as he glorified the father in his ministry on earth. He longed to take back the glory of the Godhead as he had it before the existence of the world as substantiated by John 1:1-2 (KJV)

"In the beginning was the Word, and the Word was with God, and the Word was God. The same was in the beginning with God".

It is thus implied that Jesus laid down his Godly glory to become human and to take on the mission his Father gave him. However, at the end of the mission before his crucifixion he longs to have it back as he prays in John 17:4 -5 (KJV)

"I have glorified thee on the earth: I have finished the work which thou gavest me to do. And now, O Father, glorify thou me with

thine own self with the glory which I had with thee before the world was".

The exposition of glory does not end at Gethsemane, as Jesus speaks to his second coming in many places, but here he speaks about the former glory he had that he would return with. A specific scripture that outlines this, amongst others is Matthew 24:30-31(KJV)

"And then shall appear the sign of the Son of man in heaven: and then shall all the tribes of the earth mourn, and they shall see the Son of man coming in the clouds of heaven with power and great glory. And he shall send his angels with a great sound of a trumpet, and they shall gather his elect from the four winds, from one end of heaven to the other".

When Jesus comes to reign over his kingdom, we will know him in a different glory, one we can only imagine until we see it.

Confirmation of eternity

When speaking about eternal life John 3: 16 comes to mind (KJV)

"For God so loved the world, that he gave his only begotten Son, that whosoever believeth in him should not perish, but have everlasting life".

Jesus is explicit in his teachings about two eternal positions, and there is confusion here: eternal life is termed heaven and eternal damnation termed hell. Yet, both these phenomena are eternal, therefore the souls of humans live eternally will do it in one of two places, heaven, or hell.

Eternity is confirmed by Jesus Christ himself in the four Gospels and by the Revelation of John, the last book of the Bible.

It is obvious that because God lives and exists outside of time, the eternal expanse is not known to man. Although trillions of light years in the past have become visible to man via different technologies, humankind cannot see into the future, only the past can be made visible to a certain extent. And with all the technology and knowledge available humans do still not know what they do not know, especially about eternity and immortality. Yet out of all our denial, we as humans can deny God, try to find life on other planets but we cannot deny the path of existence, which is eternal, throughout the many galaxies we have become aware of.

Therefore, in accepting the reality of eternity one needs to contemplate on God's eternal plan and not just three or four millennia which we have closely monitored with history and through science. The living presence of eternity is visible through Jesus Christ who died, was resurrected on the third day, walked on earth for 40 days and then ascended into heaven in about AD 33.

He spoke to the reality of heaven and hell which would last for eternity, confirmed by His teaching about the first and second death together with eternal life. Herein I propose Matthew 25:46 as confirmation (KJV)

"And these shall go away into everlasting punishment: but the righteous into life eternal".

However, one must not disregard Revelation 20:6 (KJV)

"Blessed and holy is he that hath part in the first resurrection: on such the second death hath no power, but they shall be priests of

God and of Christ and shall reign with him a thousand years".

Jesus at Gethsemane

Jesus' last hours at Gethsemane are well explained in each of the Gospels Matthew 26;36-46, Mark 15:32-42, Luke 22:39-46 and John 17 speaks to Jesus' last prayer known to us as the High Priestly prayer. Gethsemane is marked as the last intimate moments Jesus had with his disciples and it seems also his last disappointment as they fell asleep in his time of need.

What the first three Gospels record about Jesus' prayer is the heaviness of the cup he had to drink and whilst praying his sweat drops turning to blood. This implies the tremendous anxiety Jesus was going through whilst praying this last time before the betrayal and crucifixion. It seems that these stressful hours were only shared with him by three of his followers, Peter, James and John, the others Jesus had left to sit alone.

The true prayerful account of Jesus is in John 17 where Jesus prays intercessory prayer and delivers a "close out" report on his earthly mission. It is ironic that Jesus prays that the hour has come and that he should be glorified by the Father, one almost asks how the betrayal, judgment and crucifixion can be a glorification.

Yet Jesus speaks to the fact that God has given him power over all flesh in John 17:2, his prayer is almost in words to elevate himself above the pain which he is about to endure. In verse four of the same chapter, he concedes to finishing the work he was sent to do, but was it, bearing in mind the final stages of the work were still ahead of him, to pay the sacrificial price of sin for humankind.

In verse eight Jesus assures the Father that he had given the disciples the teachings that his Father has ordered him to do. In verse nine Jesus prays for his disciples in relation to the world they live in, and almost futuristic prayer as if he is handing over his mission to them, so that they may continue with what he was called for.

In verse 13 He prays that his joy may abound in them although he realises that the disciples are hated by those around them. Jesus prays not that they leave the world but that they be guarded from evil and that they be sanctified for their mission that Jesus sent them into the world for, the great commission. By verse 20, Jesus includes all the future converts in his prayer so that they may live in unity.

In verse 22, Jesus transfers the glory of the Father to the disciples and the future Church, wherein he calls for their future perfection. In Christ's closure, verse 26 he declares that the love of the Father be the same as the love within the disciples and the Church.

Learning from Jesus' High Priestly Payer in John, his intercession implicates the church of today, and although this event happened two thousand years ago not all the Church has realised its full capacity in Christ. What is not visible in the Gospels, except for a few instances, is Jesus' prayer life. All that is visible is that he found time alone to pray or went into retreat for prayer. What he prayed about and the content of Jesus' conversation with the Father is rather unknown. However, Jesus had the authority of heaven upon his ministry even inasmuch as forgiving sin. This is evident at most of the healings that took place throughout the four Gospels.

Jesus' prayer at Gethsemane shows us that even our prayers of anxiety should not question God. His prayers in the most anxious moments of his life were founded on his mission, his Father and what he still needed to accomplish. Although he was at the most difficult psychological moment of his life, he asked for the cup to pass but left the option to the Father. The mission and calling he did not question, neither did he question God, his position, his purpose, or his future in the prayers he prayed.

In concluding this part of the discussion, one should know how to pray in the most difficult times, the position, the purpose, and the future should be left in God's hands. One should never insult God, or his plan in our times of anxiety. Remember God is supreme, our Father created not only the earth but the entire universe and its function, he is the only God.

On the cross

The life and death moment of Jesus was on the cross of Calvary, incidentally the place of the skull, thus even where Jesus was crucified had to do with death.

On the cross even the heavenlies mourned, as darkness filled the earth for three on the day before the High Sabbath, and God the Father turns away just for this time until Jesus dies as the living Son of God, under the banner "King of the Jews". This was the most extraordinary day the universe had experienced together with the unexplained darkness even over the Olympic Games of that year (A.D. 32-33) as Phlegon of Trallesii, a Greek Historian wrote.

This moment in history explains the heart of God, for His Son and for humankind. Yet moving to the position Jesus took on the cross in prayer, it is a vital observation that it is not recorded that Jesus prayed on the cross, only his cry I refer to in Matthew 27:45-46 (KJV)

"Now from the sixth hour there was darkness over all the land unto the ninth hour. And about the ninth hour Jesus cried with a loud voice, saying, Eli, Eli, lama sabachthani, My God, my God, why hast thou forsaken me?".

Expect for his life and mission closing remarks, *"I Thirst"* as recorded in John, after which he was offered vinegar, then Jesus Died. Matthew 27:50 (KJV)

Jesus, when he had cried again with a loud voice, yielded up the ghost".

The earth's crust and the temple are affected by the death of Jesus with the miraculous moment as the Sun comes out and the darkness is broken, the Gospels record earthquakes, graves opening and dead saints coming to life.

Matthew 27:51-53 (KJV)

"And, behold, the veil of the temple was rent in twain from the top to the bottom; and the earth did quake, and the rocks rent; and the graves were opened; and many bodies of the saints which slept arose, and came out of the graves after his resurrection, and went into the holy city, and appeared unto many".

There was no prayer involved with the miraculous signs at the crucifixion and death of Jesus everything the prophets had spoken and prayed about, all Jesus had taught and prayed about, came into fulfilment as the 1st covenant closes out at the renting of the veil and the 2nd Covenant begins with the death of Christ.

What one must remember that in Jesus' worst day, that of the crucifixion, he had no time to put aside for prayer, I mean to bring this to the attention of the reader. Jesus had prayed and conversed with the father about this day, previous prayer, although he had to go through it all, had given him the strength to complete his holy mission even though it cost him his life.

In this regard, many times, whilst one is in despair, with no time to pray, just sorting out the immediate problems, the previous prayers allow one the strength and courage to go through the trial of that time. In other cases, one may have other's praying whilst one is not up to it.

Post resurrection

Surprisingly, Jesus met with his disciples and his followers after his resurrection and did this for the 40 days between the resurrection and his ascension into heaven. In many of these meetings Jesus sat down to eat with his following, like the Emmaus brethren in Luke 24:30 (KJV), I quote

"And it came to pass, as he sat at meat with them, he took bread, and blessed it, and brake, and gave to them".

In the events following the resurrection, Jesus' prayer was one of blessing for the food he ate with the disciples, it is not recorded in the Gospels or in Acts that Jesus prayed about anything else.

Interestingly though, is that whilst Jesus was visiting disciples in different places the meetings with Jesus were different, he visited his following with heavenly authority.

He appeared to them and left them supernaturally. Another wonderful experience was Jesus' last miracle, the one recorded where the disciples went to fish. Jesus suddenly appears out of nowhere, and from far tells Peter and team to cast their nets in on the other side of the boat. The nets were so full they were about to tear, it is so awe-inspiring when Jesus appears on the scene. I quote John 21:4-6 (KJV)

"But when the morning was now come, Jesus stood on the shore: but the disciples knew not that it was Jesus. Then Jesus saith unto them, Children, have ye any meat? They answered him, No.

And he said unto them, Cast the net on the right side of the ship, and ye shall find. They cast therefore, and now they were not able to draw it for the multitude of fishes".

To conclude one must peruse, Luke 24:49; John 14:16-17; 14:26, 15:26; 16:7-16, Acts 1:8; 2:1-21. Yet I quote Acts 1:4-5 (KJV) directly, a replication of Luke 24:9

"And, being assembled together with them, commanded them that they should not depart from Jerusalem, but wait for the promise of the Father, which, saith he, ye have heard of me. For John truly baptized with water; but ye shall be baptized with the Holy Ghost not many days hence".

Hence the end of Jesus' ministry fulfills the prophecy of Isaiah (44:3-4; 59:20-21) and Joel (2:28-32) about the Holy Spirit.

The disciples were advised by Jesus to wait in Jerusalem until the Holy Spirit had come upon them, one seems to question the waiting period of about ten days, did they fast and pray? were they all in the upper room all the time? Biblical text gives one a small glimpse of ten days and then the climax in Acts 2. Yet, by implication, this waiting period must have been saturated with prayer as is recorded In Acts 2:1.

Summary

I close the exposition of Jesus' ministry and prayer with a brief concluding summary to ensure that the main gist of the reading remains prevalent. The Chapter starts off with a discussion on communicating with God following with a discussion about Jesus in relation to fasting and prayer. This relates well to the exposition of Jesus' ministry in relation to the Lord's prayer. Then the discussions follow through Jesus' prayer in Gethsemane, the Crucifixion and Christ's 40 days on earth prior to the ascension. The Chapter closes with a discussion on the fulfilment of Christ's ministry and the prophets Isaiah and Joel after the ten days post Jesus' ascension. Pentecost meaning the 50th day, this is after the Passover. Symbolically a new day of the 2nd Covenant, the birth of a new Church even for gentiles. I close this Chapter with a Jesus prayer worksheet.

The Jesus Prayer Worksheet

To start with prayer analysis, try working through the model prayer Jesus proposed, interpret it, and then see how you can enhance your daily prayer journey. Take each topical point listed and see how you can build your prayer around it.

1. Our Father

2. Hallowed be thy name

3. Thy Kingdom

4. Thy will

5. Earth and heaven

6. Provision of daily bread

7. Personal forgiveness

8. Us forgiving others

9. Protection from temptation
10. Delivering us from evil influence
11. Confirmation of God's kingdom
12. Confirmation of God's power
13. Confirmation of God's Glory
14. Confirmation of eternity

CHAPTER 4
Understanding the works of prayer

Have you ever speculated about the different concepts of prayer, and why they are so important to the spiritual growth of a believer? Surely some of the concepts you may relate to are known to you by the power of your own prayers, receiving what you pray for, prayer as a spiritual job, a weapon, a source of protection and the like.

The works of prayer are intertwined between the world we live in, the spiritual realm, and with God the Father through his Son and the Holy Spirit. At the same time the works of prayer have something to do with the Angels, both of God and the fallen ones of Satan. Additionally, to understand the works of prayer I will discuss seven aspects namely:

1. Prayer as a spiritual duty
2. Prayer as a weapon
3. Prayer as a source of protection
4. Prayer in our physical world
5. Prayer in the spiritual realm
6. Prayer and the Angelic
7. Testimonies about answered prayer and miraculous intervention

In this discussion I would like to expose the intertwined reality of what happens when believers pray. This may activate imagination; however, I hope it activates your mind and spirit in a way that will cause you to take on the task of prayer, for specific results, based on Biblical principles.

Prayer as a spiritual duty

Bounds (2009) purports that prayer is not a petty duty and should not be made up of the fragments of time taken off our business of worldly engagements. Prayer according to him should not be swallowed up by church or other duties, as it should come first. By implication, the saying of Jesus, "seek ye first the Kingdom of God and all the other shall be added unto you", puts dutiful prayer first and labour of any sort second. Thus, prayer is obligatory, it is the empowering instrument that the child of God requires to survive in the spiritual turmoil of life.

If prayer does not take place, personal communication with God is non-existent, and will not enrich the relationship between God and man. This implies that the duty of prayer is far reaching as it brings about change in the heart, mind, and spirit of he/she that is praying. It is for the sake of the church of Christ that the duty of intercessory prayer is so important. Such prayer will be for loved ones, friends, family, enemies, society at large, the church, government, and leaders. In conclusion, the duty of prayer extends from the individual to the spiritual battleground.

Allow me to add that backsliding also has to do with the lack of prayer, as the foundation of spiritual life is slowly depleted, so too the other things in life become more important. One seems to cede to temptation much quicker when there is no spiritual contact with God, as if the spirit loses it vigour and will to fight sin.

Prayer as a weapon

When one goes to war, and we are at war, the weapons one takes up are the ones that one believes will earn the victory of the battle on hand. As far back as Exodus one sees prayer as a weapon, let us look at Moses, when he was deliberating with Pharaoh in Egypt to let the Israelites go. Pharaoh, an unbeliever, asks Moses to pray for the hail in Egypt to stop. Prayer, by implication, caused the stop and start of the plagues in Egypt. I quote Exodus 9:26-30 (GNB)

The region of Goshen, where the Israelites lived, was the only place where there was no hail. The king sent for Moses and Aaron and said, "This time I have sinned; the LORD is in the right, and my people and I are in the wrong.

Pray to the LORD! We have had enough of this thunder and hail! I promise to let you go; you don't have to stay here any longer." Moses said to him, "As soon as I go out of the city, I will lift up my hands in prayer to the LORD. The thunder will stop, and there will be no more hail, so that you may know that the earth belongs to the LORD. But I know that you and your officials do not yet fear the LORD God".

Prayer to God, in this case, changed the weather patterns, it was the trigger of faith to move the weaponry of God.

The apostle Paul writes to the Church in Ephesians and I quote, Ephesians 6:12 (KJV)

"*For we wrestle not against flesh and blood, but against principalities, against powers, against the rulers of the darkness of this world, against spiritual wickedness in high places*".

If this is the case, with what do we wrestle? The child of God wrestles in an unknown world through prayer against the powers and principalities of darkness. In many instances business and political plots to undermine Christian brothers and sisters, have either come to light, or have been overthrown by the prayers of the saints. It is no wonder the prophet Isaiah writes (54:17) (KJV)

"No weapon that is formed against thee shall prosper; and every tongue that shall rise against thee in judgment thou shalt condemn. This is the heritage of the servants of the LORD, and their righteousness is *of me, saith the LORD".*

This leads to my next discussion about the protection prayer brings upon children of God, in a later chapter more will be discussed on spiritual weaponry in a discussion on spiritual warfare and the battleground of the believer.

Prayer as a source of protection

Additionally, I quote the Apostle Paul, Ephesians 6:10-12 (KJV)

"Finally, my brethren, be strong in the Lord, and in the power of his might. Put on the whole armour of God, that ye may be able to stand against the wiles of the devil. For we wrestle not against flesh and blood, but against principalities, against powers, against the rulers of the darkness of this world, against spiritual wickedness in high places".

The armour of God is put on as an intertwined fabric though the power of prayer. The question one asks is, why armour and what confirms the protection we have by wearing armour?

One needs to understand that to carry armour on the body is heavy and not always easy to carry, however, the armouring is a means of protecting oneself against the fiery spiritual arrows of Satan and the demonic. In this vein, I again credit Paul on his relevance to the armour of the then Roman soldier. One should read the scripture, Ephesians 6:13-18 with a picture of a 1st century Roman Soldier in mind. For the ease of use, I quote directly from the King James version of the Bible:

"*Wherefore take unto you the whole armour of God, that ye may be able to withstand in the evil day, and having done all, to stand. Stand therefore, having your loins girt about with truth, and having on the breastplate of righteousness; And your feet shod with the preparation of the gospel of peace; Above all, taking the shield of faith, wherewith ye shall be able to quench all the fiery darts of the wicked. And take the helmet of salvation, and the sword of the Spirit, which is the word of God: Praying always with all prayer and supplication in the Spirit and watching thereunto with all perseverance and supplication for all saints".*

In verse 18, Paul amplifies the essentials of prayer, as a method of watching over the saints. Therefore, watching over our fellow believers implies protection that comes through prayer.

Moreover, prayer is a physical mode of communication that reaches across the spiritual boundaries which we cannot see and which we do not know.

As Paul writes to the Ephesians, he wants them to relate to the Roman soldiers they know, yet our weaponry is much different, I wonder how we could relate prayer to sending missiles into the enemy's camp, or rockets, even spiritual surveillance. We have become so knowledgeable and modern, but as millennials we forget to see how powerful the prayer arsenal of the Kingdom of God really should be.

Do yourself a favour and watch some of the children's programmes on television, see how magic is dished up for the little ones as truth, yet we fail to prove more power to them through our prayers.

Prayer in our physical world

As much as prayer is spiritual, it is also physical and has the power to change things in the natural world where we live. In this I point to often unbelievable occurrences that come through prayer. It is by faith and prayer that situations which affect us drastically, can change in a moment.

I have heard many believers say, "I am a realist", does this exclude them from the prayer that can change their position in life? Absolutely not, when a believer prays, even the realist discovers how real God is. If anything, prayer is proven through the supernatural into the natural world, where we work, play, live and survive. No matter how big or small the situation, God hears our prayers and allows for the solutions to happen, sometimes through people, other times it is a miracle that goes against science and realism.

A good example of a supernatural intervention is where Paul and Silas, in jail bound by chains, in barred cells started signing and praying. God heard their prayer and praises and he freed them in a natural, supernatural way. I quote Acts 16:25-26 (KJV)

"And at midnight Paul and Silas prayed, and sang praises unto God: and the prisoners heard them. And suddenly there was a great earthquake, so that the foundations of the prison were shaken: and

immediately all the doors were opened, and every one's bands were loosed".

I often ask why believers think that these kinds of miracles are outside of their reach. What I have learned is that a believer, when in deep trouble, and they have no way out, and when they turn to God with their whole being, He hears and changes their circumstances for them. What believers do not always see, is what happens in the spiritual realm when they pray.

Prayer in the spiritual realm

The spiritual realm consists of the Holy Spirit living in and around us, supreme above all. Yet the spiritual realm, except for the power of discernment, is mostly rather closed to most believers. They would not see the Angelic, or the demonic, Satan and the like. We were granted a free pass to enter this spiritual realm through the Holy Spirit. Our spiritual chaperone was God's promise and Jesus' confirmation in Luke11:13 (KJV)

"If ye then, being evil, know how to give good gifts unto your children: how much more shall your heavenly Father give the Holy Spirit to them that ask him?".

Then the Psalmist also says in Psalm 51:11(KJV)

"Cast me not away from thy presence; and take not thy holy spirit from me".

Therefore, the Holy Spirit is not such a new idea, as the Holy Spirit has been around as long as the Father and the Son in trinity and is still the most important companion a believer has.

Besides the aforesaid, the Angelic and the demonic were created by God, just as the human was, I quote Psalm 8:4-5(KJV)

"What is man, that thou art mindful of him? and the son of man, that thou visitest him? For thou hast made him a little lower than the angels, and hast crowned him with glory and honour".

Now, Lucifer on the other hand was an Archangel and the worshipper together with legions of angels but fallen as referenced in Isaiah 14:12-15 (KJV)

"How art thou fallen from heaven, O Lucifer, son of the morning! how art thou cut down to the ground, which didst weaken the nations! For thou hast said in thine heart, I will ascend into heaven, I will exalt my throne above the stars of God: I will sit also upon the mount of the congregation, in the sides of the north: I will ascend above the heights of the clouds; I will be like the Most High. Yet thou shalt be brought down to hell, to the sides of the pit".

Therefore, demons are fallen angels, once glorifying God, then cast out of heaven with Satan.

One asks how relevant this is to the spiritual world? So much so that the demonic is as present as the Angelic and, if I may say, the Holy Spirit. The demonic seek human bodies to live in, as this body gives it form and identity as they are metamorphic, Jesus sent them into pigs. More than one demon can take possession of a human being, such a case was when Jesus freed one man of more than a thousand demons. For this I quote Mark 5:7-13 (KJV)

"And cried with a loud voice, and said, what have I to do with thee, Jesus, thou Son of the most high God? I adjure thee by God, that thou torment me not. For he said unto him, Come out of the man, thou unclean spirit. And he asked him, what is thy name? And he answered, saying, my name is *Legion: for we are many. And he*

besought him much that he would not send them away out of the country. Now there was there nigh unto the mountains a great herd of swine feeding. And all the devils besought him, saying, send us into the swine, that we may enter them. And forthwith Jesus gave them leave. And the unclean spirits went out and entered the swine: and the herd ran violently down a steep place into the sea, (they were about two thousand) and were choked in the sea".

One can safely say that there is Angelic and demonic movement in the spiritual realm at all hours of the day and these are not visible to the human eye. However, it is God's desire that the Holy Spirit lead and guide us in all our ways. Nevertheless, at different stages of life one could encounter the demonic, especially when the Holy Spirit is present and by discernment exposes it. Therefore, entering the spiritual realm should not be feared. However, I include that the spiritual realm should be approached with caution and it can be regarded as a spiritual battlefield too.

To this end I quote the Apostle Paul in his first letter to the Corinthian congregation: verses 2:12-14 (KJV)

"Now we have received, not the spirit of the world, but the spirit which is of God; that we might know the things that are freely given to us of God. Which things also we speak, not in the words which man's wisdom teacheth, but which the Holy Ghost teacheth, comparing spiritual things with spiritual. But the natural man receiveth not the things of the Spirit of God: for they are foolishness unto him: neither can he know them, because they are spiritually discerned".

As I have mentioned previously, the spiritual realm should be where we worship, glorify and experience God. Yet many believers, instead of seeking God's glory, use the spiritual to rather find and learn more about Satan's work. This has two implications, they look for Satan and the demonic in every situation and even worse, through their devil hunting they miss the glory of God.

Notwithstanding my previous comment, I want to state emphatically that the believer, (Mark 16:17) should when discerning the demonic, drive them out, to free those who are bound in their spirits.

Just before my sermon on a Sunday evening around the year 2000, a local club bouncer entered the church and sat in an empty middle pew. The pew was about five meters in length, we were singing about the blood of Jesus when the demonic revealed itself in the man, he screamed and overturned the pew that was well bolted to the floor. He ran out of the Church where a passing missionary, met him at the door and drove several demons out of him. We did not look for the demons, but the power of God reveals them, has the church not lost its discerning power? Certainly, the devil fears the blood of Jesus Christ, and he fears those believers who administer it, as much as the precious blood itself.

It is odd how in the post-millennial church the overriding action, or victory of the believer over the demonic has decreased. Is it not that the fiery prayer of the believer has diminished to a tick in the box exercise, or pushed over as an expectation for specific intercessors or prayer warriors? If believers live by the spirit, the devil will fear their appearance on his battlefield, because they will enter it with the power, glory, and honour of Christ.

Before I address the Angelic, I would like to encourage the reader to know that the believer's life and experiences ought to be spiritual, and this will be different to what sciences and schools of thought teach us. Different schools of thought bring us into direct contact with the New Age works of the Devil. Though I have studied Psychology and believe there is truth in theory that builds up the mind and identifies problems. Nonetheless I fear many are being led away from God to serve the power of darkness by meditation, welcoming evil spirits as mentors and dabbling in Eastern Idolatry and the like. Consequently, before I discuss the Angelic,

I warn that many so-called angels that have been identified are not heavenly beings, they are metamorphic demons who come as angels of light but represent the order of darkness.

Prayer and the Angelic

Irrespective what cults or other religions teach, our Bible only speaks to three Archangels, Michael, Gabriel and the fallen one Lucifer. Luke 1:19 (KJV) the Angel Gabriel appears to Zachariah, the Mary in Luke 1:23 and specifically introduces himself as

"I am Gabriel, that stands in the presence of God".

Lucifer I have discussed as the fallen angel (Isaiah 14:12-14, Job 1:7-12, 2:1-7), lastly Michael we read about in Daniel and in Revelation as the Angel that goes to war for God (Daniel 10:13,21; Jude 1:9 and Revelation 12:7).

Now I have the following theory about the Angelic, these are real beings created by God. There are Cherubim and Seraphim that are heavenly beings. Yet Satan and

Jesus both agree that God sends angels to protect God's children, this is when Jesus was tempted by Satan after his fast. What emanates from Jesus' discussion with Satan is that Jesus by not speaking against the Angelic, both the Son of God and Satan understood the spiritual world well, that Angels do exist for the protection of the believer. I quote Matthew 4:6&7 (GNB)

"and said to him, "If you are God's Son, throw yourself down, for the scripture says, 'God will give orders to his angels about you; they will hold you up with their hands, so that not even your feet will be hurt on the stones". Jesus answered, "But the scripture also says, 'Do not put the Lord your God to the test".

My theory extrapolates the following from scripture about the Angelic realm, it is under the command of the Father through two Archangels, Michael, and Gabriel, these could command the Cherubim and

Seraphim. The service of angels is not propelled by the believer's prayer, but directly from God's throne. Conversely the Holy Spirit and the believer have direct contact with God the Father through the Son. Likewise, when God decides there should be Angelic intervention it is commanded via the Angelic hierarchy to propel a solution for a believer who is in some sort of trouble.

So how does prayer fit into the service of the Angelic? Prayer is the one stop shop, so together with faith and a good sincere attitude the believer receives the service of Angels when the Father commands such. In closing, believers cannot command the Angelic, but they have the power and authority of Christ to renounce the demonic, and to command them to leave any area or body.

Testimonies about answered prayer and miracles

As a pastor I have had so many answered prayers, I cannot list all the testimonies here. Yet, I would rather list miracles outside of just the day-to-day prayers that God has answered. One must not forget that answered prayer happens several times in a day. Just give my statement some thought; one starts to pray in the morning and asks God to protect loved ones, at the end of the day no bad incident had occurred, how many times in that day were our loved ones possibly in danger?

One could also pray for solutions to situations out of one's control, the solution comes automatically without and personal intervention, this is answered prayer.

I guess the miracles we look for our right under our noses, we are so used to them we don't even notice them anymore.

Testimony 1

Several years ago, I was called by my pastor colleague's wife to come and say the final prayer, her husband was dying of prostate cancer. I met the family in the waiting room where they asked me to please bury Pastor Daniel when he passes-away on that day. I went to the pastor, my friend, on the mobile stretcher, covered with a mask and theatre blanket. I bent down and asked him in his ear if he believed that God could still heal him. He nodded, and I prayed that God would intervene.

I left the hospital that day, despondent, upset and said "Lord, I'm tired of seeing people off before they die, I need the healing power of God to work when I pray". The pastor's wife phoned me the next morning, says she does not know how it happened, the professor came in and said this case must be turned around immediately. Pastor Daniel recovered from almost dead to a walking man in several weeks.

One Sunday, about two years later, I was preaching one morning at our church in Centurion. I testified about this miracle in my sermon, when I looked up Pastor Daniel entered the door of our church that morning. This is a miracle upon a miracle, first his healing, then he walks into the church at the right time as I was testifying about him.

My God is great and what is better is that the miracle was confirmed that morning to persons who may not have believed in supernatural healing.

Testimony 2

In 2010 the Lord woke me one night and laid on my heart that I should put up a 500-seater tent and host services every day for 40 days. I woke my wife, shared this with her, she said we may have to apply for a loan then, we both agreed that if God had woken me with this vision it should be done. At that time, our congregation was five years old, we were having our Sunday services in a school hall close to our house.

That same Sunday morning, I stood to give my sermon and announced that God had spoken to me in the night and that the congregation should prepare for a 40-day revival campaign in a tent. I said I do not know where the tent will come from, but God said it and I believed it.

After the service I was greeting congregants at the door of the hall when an elderly man called me one side. He asked how old I was, I shared my age with him. His answer was, I could have been your father. Then he asked, "and how many seats must this tent have?" I replied, about five hundred. He nodded and said, "I have a blue and white tent with 500 chairs for you, when do you want to put it up?".

My God is a "same day" delivery God. We put up the tent, had a wonderful 40 days of revival services based on Rick Warren's 40 days purpose driven life. The results were magnificent, church growth and the tent and chairs were donated to us. In 2011 we moved to a piece of farmland on the outskirts of Centurion where the tent was our Church until November 2015. I want to use this testimony to show the reader that our journey of purpose also has setbacks that take us into a new season or dimension of life.

In 2015 we celebrated our tenth birthday in the tent, and we invited Dr Landman, federal chair of the Pentecostal Protestant Church, to do the celebration sermon. He walked up to me and said, "sometimes we need to start over, you've come 10 years and God says, time to start again". This was rather a shocking message to hear when we showcased our proposed church and site development plans. Each of our board and the architect gave a speech after the service and spoke about a school and church that would be built. This was in March 2015. In November 2015 I attended a conference in London and when I returned the board members took me to the tent and shared the bad news, the wind had ripped the tent to pieces, beyond repair. That Sunday morning, we had our last service inside a very badly damaged tent. After the service we packed up, folded up and stored what we could, the restart button was pushed as Dr Landman prophesied seven months earlier. Consequently, we downsized from our five hundred-seater-tent in one month, to a veranda of a house.

This unforeseeable situation forced us to change our place of worship in November and December of that year. On the 31st December 2015 we opened our very small Shalom Barn, a church which could barely seat 60 people. We started over again, was this discouraging, o yes, I will not deny that this was probably the worst time of my entire ministry, it humbled me in many ways, however it was a building block for the future of Shalom Christian Church. This event really stifled church growth due to the look and feel of this little place we had to make do with for our Sunday services.

In January 2016 we started building the side hall of our auditorium in faith. At this stage we had a 72-month lease on the ground which lapsed at the end of September 2017. To make the ground ours we required and amount of 1.7 million Rand. We had to choose, build in faith, or wait for the ground to be paid. We, about four of us, chose the route of faith, for which I was well criticised, to build and then trust in God for the settlement of the ground. The road of faith is not easy, it is ridiculed, and it is a lonely place to be. Nevertheless, we started building, at this time I had three supporters and many critics. My supporters worked hard to get the cash to build, banks in South Africa are reluctant to furnish churches with loans. We set out to build our side hall for R1.2 million Rand. Prayer was the cornerstone of every payment we made. My wife said, after one service, "you never asked for money at Church before, please stop asking".

At this stage, August 2017, the cash dried up, we had a building that was almost complete, but it was useable, no carpets, unfinished ceiling and a concrete roof that had not been sealed. We opened and ordained the side hall for service on 17 October 2017. Everything that was built was paid for, in cash with seating space of about 200.

Although we had the building, the Landlord wanted to change the lease and sale conditions and wanted to increase the price of the land with another R1.4 million. I prayed together with others and bargained with the Landlord about conditions to keep the land price the same. The conditions were that the site development plans for the entire phase be passed by the municipality on 30 December 2019, that a bond be placed in the name of the Church, with me as leader by the same date, and that the development fees of R220 000.00 be paid to the municipality in November 2017. If these conditions were not met, the land and the church buildings remain the property of the Landlord.

This was a tall order, we needed R1.92 million in cash by 15 December 2017, as all banks and businesses close for the Christmas holidays. At this time my faith, more than anyone else's was put to the test, it was only God who could make this work for us.

On the 14th of November 2017, the church was granted an interest free loan to pay the municipal development fees of R220 000. On the 7th of December 2010 bond was registered for R1.7 million with a condition that the Church would not pay the amount back to the Pentecostal Protestant Church unless the property was sold, that meant that the property was paid in full except for the transfer fees.

On the 10th of December 2017, the Site Development Plans were passed by the Municipality meaning that all the conditions of sale had been fulfilled and that the registration process could continue. This process ended in June of 2018 and the property is registered in the name of Shalom Christian Church, a congregation of the Pentecostal Protestant Church of South Africa. In November 2019, the loan was paid in full and the property, the building and all its moveable assets were paid without the church owing anyone any monies.

Testimony 3

The problem we had with the new building and being cash strapped, was the concrete roof leaked like a sift. It did not matter what we did, after each rainstorm the water would seep through the concrete roof. I consulted engineers on specific fiber paint coatings and found a suitable compound. One morning I sat in the church looking at a drum of the fiber compound, reading its instructions I worked out the volume that would be required, at that stage I only had three drums of the paint. I worked out the volume and the cost and I realised we required about R10 000 to complete the sealing project, which we did not have.

I prayed and left the church, about fifteen minutes later I called a fellow pastor and whilst speaking to him he said "by the way, send me the churches account number, we will be donating R10 000 toward the roof sealing of your church. God answered a prayer in 15 minutes.

Testimony 4

In August of 2019, the Lord again woke me with a dream and laid on my heart to start a school in 2018. Again, I announced it in faith on the Sunday morning, first to the pastors, then later the same morning to the congregation. There was excitement in the air, you could sense the happiness about the matter. A month later I started fasting after I worked out what start-up capital would be required, and I knew we did not have R268 000 at all.

I started fasting and within the first seven days of my fast I got an SMS from a congregation member. It was a bank notification of a R250 000 bank transfer into the Church's account. Now I want to explain the mathematics, after November we have about R18 000 free to add to the start-up capital plus the R250 000 which equals the R268 000 which I asked for. God hears the detail of our prayer. The other R18 000 was available in the normal church funds.

Testimony 5

Covid-19 came as a sudden shock in January of 2020 with a hard Lockdown from end March of the same year, Nations were in shock and turmoil, aircraft grounded, streets and highways once bustling with bumper-to-bumper traffic, all quiet. The voice of the Church was heard above the panic and suddenly media started filling up with end time warnings, I too wrote an article COVID-19 and the end times, spoke on the third awakening and the like.

Again, we prayed, and God gave us media platforms to use such as Zoom, Facebook and YouTube. We had to act quickly as our services were closed by legislation. We were live in the first week with our first service, although we were ready, we did not have all the technology built in for purpose, we then used our cell phones and Wi-Fi networks.

One may ask what prayer had to do with the COVID-19 Pandemic and the Church. Well one needed to face the following problems as a pastor:

1. Church service closed for a then unknown time.
2. Traditional income via collections fell away.
3. Members had the ability to test as many other churches as possible, that their access to media would allow.
4. Infected congregants.
5. People in the congregation with no income or food.
6. Financial losses.
7. Committed salaries that had to be paid.
8. Building upkeep with no assistance.
9. A change in the way the Church was operating.

Here is what transpired after prayer and action, we had our Easter services on-line with worship songs, lyrics, and the like. Our staff were paid their salaries, the church building lawns were maintained by a person living close by.

We prayed for those who were infected by the virus, by December 2020 the congregation had 5 Covid-19 infections of which one was severe. We had recorded no financial losses and received our collections via internet banking, and we were able to pay our church tithes. Our congregation was able to support and distributed food and necessities those in need and to assist people in getting their own businesses to function again.

The outcome of COVID-19 for our congregation was positive, we had increased our global footprint by means of social media and internet radio. Shalom Centurion now has a virtual membership together with the conventional church members who actively attend live services. The church was turned around to become a studio for live recordings, with a multi camera system for broadcasting at least two live services per week. The praise and worship and media team had doubled. A sense of Holy Spirit revival has been cultivated to take on the Revival wave when it passes over our City and Country as prophesied.

I have used these factual testimonies to explain how God works in mysterious to provide in time of need. When one works within God's calling and vision, God blesses us for the good of the body of Christ. The problem many pastors have, and I made this mistake, is they make what belongs to God their own. In this I mean God's property, the church, and its assets.

Once I realised that the Church, its buildings, and belongings were not mine, God blessed the ministry with the assets we required and more. Unfortunately, pastors sidestep their calling by doing their own business in God's house, another mistake I made. Once a pastor hands back to God, what is God's, He works on our behalf because we are but the managers or stewards of Christ's kingdom and its belongings.

This probably leads to a question, "does the church actually require assets and buildings? To this end I do acknowledge the need for assets such as the buildings, although not a spiritual requirement, they bring about a place of belonging for the children of God. Therefore, the assets of the kingdom bring about instruments of worship and places where the sinner can meet up with Jesus. Yet, with all this said, no pastor can take credit for the property of God, knowing that the same property will stay behind as a monument and will not be a reason a pastor will go to heaven. Therefor I strengthen my argument by the knowledge that Jesus says he is preparing a heavenly asset for each of us in Joh 14:2-3 "In my Father's house are many mansions: if it were not so, I would have told you. I go to prepare a place for you. And if I go and prepare a place for you, I will come again, and receive you unto myself; that where I am, *there* ye may be also. I continue with my discussion on the importance of adding fasting to prayer.

I have listed topical issues discussed in this chapter. The exercises should be done in short paragraphs suggesting changes and ways to influence your prayer life and understanding of prayer, see assignment 3, Spiritual duty.

Assignment – Prayer as a spiritual duty

1. How do I implement prayer as my spiritual duty?
2. Name at least five ways in your life where prayer can be used as a weapon
3. How can prayer be used as a source of spiritual and bodily protection?
4. Name ways in which prayer has brought about change in and around you, your job, studies, career, and family.
5. What is the difference between praying in the spirit versus praying in the spiritual realm?
6. What can be said about prayer and the Prayer Angelic
7. Give at least five examples, no matter how small, where your specific prayers were answered.

CHAPTER 5

Adding fasting to prayer

From the Old, right into the New Testament fasting has been evident for a number of reasons, and the first fast is ordered and implied by God when He instituted the day of atonement through Moses in Leviticus 16:29-31 (KJV)

"And this shall be a statute forever unto you: that in the seventh month, on the tenth day of the month, ye shall afflict your souls, and do no work at all, whether it be one of your own country, or a stranger that sojourneth among you: For on that day shall the priest make an atonement for you, to cleanse you, that ye may be clean from all

your sins before the Lord. It shall be a sabbath of rest unto you, and ye shall afflict your souls, by a statute forever".

The significance of the word forever is twofold, one the Jewish nation celebrates Yon Kippur and keep doing it year on year because of God announcing an eternal action that was required for soul cleansing. What the Israelites fail to see is that Christ had taken on the eternal atonement and it is accounted for all who receive eternal life through Christ, the lamb without blemish, slain for the atonement of sin on Mount Calvary.

By implication, the word forever is fulfilled through Christ Jesus who allows for atonement of sin at any time a person repents of his/her sin. The atoning grace of God is made manifest in the soul of the believer by the Holy Spirit of God. Therefore, one concludes that the first reason for fasting was for atonement and the humbling of one's soul before God.

The second fast that was significant in the Old Testament was the fast of David in Samuel 12:21-23 (KJV), and I quote

"*Then said his servants unto him, what thing is this that thou hast done? thou didst fast and weep for the child, while it was alive; but when the child was dead, thou didst rise and eat bread. And he said, While the child was yet alive, I fasted and wept: for I said, who can tell whether GOD will be gracious to me, that the child may live? But now he is dead, wherefore should I fast? can I bring him back again? I shall go to him, but he shall not return to me*".

David took on a fast to do two things, one to show God that he was sorry about his adultery, and secondly that God would save his son who was born through adultery. The lesson that is left for the church out of this is that David did not deny God after his son died, he somehow knew that God was in control and that his fast was not in vain. Now let us look deeper into the situation if this son of adultery lived on it would have affected the linage of Christ.

However, God gives David another Son, Solomon to take up the throne and to ensure a linage that is not construed with adultery. Was the fast of David in vain? No, I believe it caused two things, God's grace to befall him and a future solution.

Thus, one should be reminded that fasting and prayer bring us into God's plan and will for our future. Sometimes one will fast and not see immediate results, yet days, months or even years after you look back and know that God answered and changed our expected result into something better.

As a young pastor, just out of training. At this time, I felt frustrated and wanted so much to have my own congregation and ministry. I fasted and prayed for outcome and tried everything just to have a ministry that was worth my while, and of course, one that suited my style. Most newly ordained pastors feel this way.

Praying about my situation, I got word that I would be a pastor in the east, this was my answer and eventually I would belong somewhere. I measured the distance to the Middle East, Far East, even looked at Maputo being not that far East. With all this measurement and planning, I soon learnt that if God says east, one should not try to run out ahead of him, my east was much closer that I had expected.

Just after this I led a service at the congregation where I was assistant pastor, Montana, and the Holy Spirit moved that morning, I felt God in the place and so did everyone else. After Church I was invited for lunch by the Presiding Pastor, Dr Deon

Stassen. After lunch we had a conversation about a church planting in an eastern suburb of Pretoria, I had Garsfontein in mind, conversely, he had Rooihuiskraal in mind. Rooihuiskraal North was exactly one block up the street from my house. We had a long discussion about a Shalom Campus in this suburb, and after all the discussion I agreed to be the pastor of the new campus in my mind Garsfontein. Driving home, it hit me like a ton of bricks that I had committed to doing exactly what I had not planned, reminding myself that I wanted to be a pastor in the East of Pretoria.

Taking lessons from this situation is inevitable as God sometimes gets us into a position where commitment is eminent, like driving in a two-lane road that becomes a single lane, you slow down, and you keep going. The call to start a Shalom campus in Centurion was formalised and the journey started.

Again, I planned to start at the showgrounds in the South-west of Rooihuiskraal. However, when we had our opening meeting at the showgrounds I was met with much dissatisfaction and was asked by the then founding members to find another place. Literally speaking, God's plan is better. My wife phoned the Bakenkop Primary School to enquire about the availability of their school hall, I note this was previously not available. The school office notified us that another church had just cancelled their longstanding contract for the hall, and that they were willing to enter a contract with Shalom for Sunday services.

The humour of the story is that the hall is situated two blocks east of my house. I started a congregation to the east of where I live. God does not make mistakes and fasting brings us into alignment with God's greater plan for us. Herewith, I quote a single scripture from Isaiah 14:24 (KJV)

"The LORD of hosts hath sworn, saying, Surely as I have thought, so shall it come to pass; and as I have purposed, so shall it stand".

There is no doubt in my mind that fasting brings results, however, what I have experienced through many years, that although fasting is a spiritual activity, it has no meaning at all when it becomes a weekly ritual. To further explain, a ritual is as described by the Merriam-Webster dictionary (2019) as a sequence of activities involving gestures, words, and objects prescribed in tradition, government, and religion. I add that fasting has become a ritual of most religions, including Christianity.

The danger of doing fasting as a ritual is that it loses it spiritual power and becomes something that is done as a habit.

In this explanation I do not want to deter anyone from fasting, albeit I want to encourage people of God to fast in a way that is holy and consecrated to Him. In all of this I promote fasting for believers, and it works.

Kinds of fasting

Traditional no food no water fast – This kind of fast has been the traditional fast for people although fasting without water is extremely dangerous and is only recommended for not longer than a day. However, it is not clear whether Moses drank water in his 40 days on the mountain with God, or not, if he did not, it adds to the supernatural power that fasting brings to maintaining vital organs for which water is crucial. A person can only survive without water for a period of three to five days (4).

Thus, the so called "dry fast" is extremely dangerous and it is practiced by very few.

No food fast – The most common fast known to most is one where a person does not consume any food for a period, whilst drinking water whenever he/she is hungry. The idea is to replace meals with prayer, and contrary to opinion, it is not seen as a hunger strike or induced starvation. My late mother and father used to fast for full 40 days without consuming any foodstuff.

Nonetheless, this is a very faithful and spiritual fast that not all can do. They both lived a full 78 years and the Lord blessed them and others whilst they fasted, they believed that the no food fast was the only way.

In my opinion, the problem with the believer of today, is that they lack spiritual endurance because it is probably not taught in their church. Added to my previous comment, is that without spiritual endurance there is less spiritual growth leading to a lower level of spiritual maturity in the church, even other consequences for the church and believer. Nevertheless, fasting without eating brings much spiritual reward and God knows the heart or mind of the person fasting, his/her attitude toward God in a time of humbling brings about a spiritual and carnal blessing. This blessing and power transforms not only the individual but changes and protects the area around those who were fasting. Even situations may turn around drastically, many kilometers away, due to the faith and endurance of a believer trusting God for change.

No meat fast – This fast is often brought into context with other religions as well as Catholicism, where meat is not eaten on certain days or seasons, and so doing brought into disrepute by believers condemning such fasts due to their origin. Yet I will not be defending any religious order of fasting, I will rather concentrate on the Daniel Fast, usually of 21 days, where no meat or animal fat or produce is consumed. Contrary to [5], this fast is not a Vegan [6] one, it is Biblical.

Let's approach the fast where it started in the book of Daniel 1:11-13 (KJV)

"*Then said Daniel to Melzar, whom the prince of the eunuchs had set over Daniel, Hananiah, Mishael, and Azariah, Prove thy servants, I beseech thee, ten days; and let them give us pulse to eat, and water to drink. Then let our countenances be looked upon before thee, and the countenance of the children that eat of the portion of the king's meat: and as thou seest, deal with thy servants*".

The food prescribed by Daniel was pulse and water. Pulse in Hebrew זֵרָעֹן זֵרֹעַ

zêrôa' or zêrâ'ôn, defined from Strongs H2232 as "something sown (only in the plural), that is, a vegetable (as food): -pulse". Thus, one should also bring into context that the vegetables that are to be consumed originate from seed. Therefore, the Daniel diet is one consisting of fresh vegetables peas, beans, squash, marrow, melon, nuts, lettuce, cabbage, carrots, beet, turnips and the like. This does not include any animal products at all i.e., meat, milk, eggs, cheese and the like are not part of the diet that was proposed by Daniel for his men. Therefore, in the first book of Daniel, the challenge was a diet of vegetables and water to prove a point to the King. Notably, the King's table was full of unclean foodstuff which the Jewish men could not consume.

The second instance in scripture that has been utilised for the timing of the Daniel fast is in Daniel 10:2-3 (KJV)

"In those days I Daniel was mourning three full weeks. I ate no pleasant bread, neither came flesh nor wine in my mouth, neither did I anoint myself at all, till three whole weeks were fulfilled".

In the book of Daniel, we have two times to contend with: one, a diet of ten days, and two, a fast of 21 days.

Similarly, we have two different concepts to deal with, a diet which was a challenge between the King and the Jewish boys, and secondly a fast which for a humbling spiritual purpose. To juxtapose two scenarios, one should realise that a diet is not a fast, yet both have a specific purpose. The Daniel 1 the diet was to fix and mould the body and in Daniel 10 the fast was to fix and mould the spirit.

Therefore, one can conclude that a diet is solely for the repair and improvement of physical health, whereas a fast is taken on to bring the body into a state of humility to improve, build and capitilise on the spiritual. Finally, the diet was for a duration of 10 days and the fast for three weeks, 21 days.

One finds that believers are practicing ten- and twenty-one-day Daniel fasts. My question is, does the timespan really matter that much? Probably, what is more important is the attitude of the believer not the time he or she feels led to fast for. After all, in many instances, the Holy Spirit does lead people into a time of fasting. I have on several occasions not known why I have the urge to fast, or to call out one in the congregation, yet after time the reason does get revealed. In most cases it was precautionary and for a new season spiritual to start.

Going back to Daniel's twenty-one day fast, it was after he had the vision in Chapter 9. Daniel was confessing his sin and that of Israel and praying for Jerusalem. In his prayer he refers to the holy mountain of God, the one where Jesus will reappear as the Messiah where he ascended in Acts 1. Then the Archangel Gabriel appears and gives Daniel the vision of the end times, the seven years of tribulation. He went into a mourning fast, a period of three weeks, for the people of Israel. It is eminent that what he saw, and what was shared with him by Gabriel, was extremely upsetting.

Thus, the context of the Daniel fast needs to be understood by the believer before quoting the fast, as a fast for change, it was rather a fast of humility and a kind of mourning about the future he saw in the vision.

No beverage fast – I had authored this fast in a 40-day evangelisation campaign, and it worked. I felt the congregation needed to be united around the fasting principle. Knowing well not everyone would last 40 days on a fast, and I wanted to include as many as possible, I felt led to call a "drink water only" for 40 days. Again, this is not a diet, if you lose weight on it, and you will, it is a bonus. The congregation joined me in cutting out all beverages for 40 days, they had their normal meals yet only drank water, no coffee, tea, milk, soda or the like. It brought the entire congregation together in spiritual unity as it even involved children and teens.

Health and Fasting

Although fasting is extremely important one should also know that there are dangers and blessings in a mixed bag. Some scientist praise fasting for it's haling and cleansing characteristics, others will condemn it outright. Clark [7] advocates fasting as a fix for the body which leads to a healthier lifestyle. So too I quote Knapton [8] "Fasting for as little as three days can regenerate the entire immune system, even in the elderly, scientists have found in a breakthrough described as "remarkable". research suggests starving the body kick-starts stem cells into producing new white blood cells which fight off infection". His research was done with cancer patients.

Yet contrary to the previous researchers, Jarvis [9] speaks out against fasting and shows cases that have resulted in fatalities. I do not doubt for one moment that there are cases where fasting rituals have resulted in death. He goes further to state, and I quote "*the body cannot differentiate between voluntary fasting and starvation and deaths have occurred even with medically supervised fasts and near-fasts. People who survive prolonged fasts (starvation) may suffer anemia, decreased immunity, osteoporosis, kidney damage, or liver damage. Depressed gastrointestinal or digestive functions may persist for weeks or months. The worst thing about fasting is its destruction of lean and vital tissue needed for a healthy and active life*"

Now the sad news is, I have expereinced that pastors that have overfasted had died of organ failure. It seems that stomach acid has much to do with the breaking down of the stomach walls and intestines. Thus my warning about fasting is to not overdo it, fast for purpose and not to please others. God does not expect you to starve for His cause, He is able and mighty enough to sort out any problem without his children hurting themselves through self neglect. Fasting for days without drinking water can lead to dehidration and even organ failure [(9)].

I conclude that fasting is a powerful mecahnism when combined with prayer. Therefore the believer should understand that God never lets us down. Fasting with a wrong attitude can cause a person physical damage and even derail them spiritually and one must know that humilty is good ingredient in the fasting recipe. Jesus says that when one fasts, he/she should not talk or boast about it but should rather seek heavenly reward. I quote Jesus' teaching in Matthew 6:16-18 (KJV)

"Moreover when ye fast, be not, as the hypocrites, of a sad countenance: for they disfigure their faces, that they may appear unto men to fast. Verily I say unto you, they have their reward. But thou, when thou fastest, anoint thine head, and wash thy face; that thou appear not unto men to fast, but unto thy Father which is in secret: and thy Father, which seeth in secret, shall reward thee openly".

See how you can make fasting work in your prayer life by doing the next assignment.

Assignment: Fasting

1. Why do believers fast?
2. Does Christian fasting relate in any way to fasting in other religions including New Age detoxing?
3. Why would you combine fasting to your prayer time, and what would the objectives be for your next fast?
4. Name at least three kinds of fast which can suite you.
5. If you have fasted before, what testimonies do you have because of it?
6. What should one be careful of in respect of one's health when fasting?
7. If you were asked to arrange a fasting and prayer chain at your church, how would you go about it?

CHAPTER 6

The Holy Spirit and prayer

Just as the Holy Spirit is active in the Holy trinity with the Father and the Son of God, so it cannot be less active in prayer. The Holy Spirit and prayer are inseparable, and Jesus confirms this in his reasoning with the lady at the well in John 4:23-24 (KJV)

"*But the hour cometh, and now is, when the true worshippers shall worship the Father in spirit and in truth: for the Father seeketh such to worship him. God is a Spirit: and they that worship him must worship him in spirit and in truth*".

The implication from the latter scripture is that worship, which includes prayer, is very spiritual and secondly, it is interrelated with truth. This further infers that if one worships God, then there must be a spiritual medium or channel through which one should approach the Godhead.

To shed more light on the previous discussion I refer to Jesus' promise of the Holy Spirit as seen in John 15:26 (KJV)

"*But when the Comforter is come, whom I will send unto you from the Father, even the Spirit of truth, which proceedeth from the Father, he shall testify of me*".

Here Jesus also calls the Holy Spirit, the Spirit of truth and is confirmed by John 16:13-14 (KJV)

"*Howbeit when he, the Spirit of truth, is come, he will guide you into all truth: for he shall not speak of himself; but whatsoever he shall hear, that shall he speak, and he will shew you things to come. He shall glorify me: for he shall receive of mine and shall shew it unto you".*

This signifies that what Jesus wants to share with the Church, and or the individual, shall be conveyed by the Holy Spirit to the receptor, i.e., the child of God. Yet one needs to understand where the triune God speaks into the human soul or mind through its spirit. The key lies in the first scripture John 4:23-24, in two aspects, spirit and truth. To this end one must understand the triune composition of the human, body, soul or mind and spirit.

The spirit of the human is the breath of God, in Greek *πνεῦμα pneuma* pronounced *pnyoo'-mah* (Strongs G4151) and in Hebrew רוּחַrûach phonetically pronounced *roo*'-akh (Strongs H7306/7). I will not *attempt to go into theological detail or delve into the Biblical origin, in which many Scholars have done well. However, I use these words to bring about unity between, the creational breath of God, the human spirit, and the Holy Spirit.*

Bringing the two words into perspective, let us understand rûach as the breath of God, which every human receives at birth. Because God is everlasting, by implication His breath will be too. This means that the spirit that lives in a human, as God's life-giving breath, shall not die. The unfortunate fact being that if this is the case, each human spirit shall live for eternity.

Thus, eternal life means an eternal presence with or without God. Therefore, although the spirit of the unsaved soul does not die, eternal damnation or second death means an eternity away from the presence of God. The mere fact of an eternal place away from God is very scary and unknown, all we know is that Jesus refers to a bottomless pit and outer darkness (Matthew 8:12; 22:13; 25:30) with Revelation referring to the bottomless pit (Revelation 9:1,2,11; 11:7; 17:8; 20:1; 20:3).

I will never forget an outer darkness fall simulation I was on in Disneyworld, Orlando in 2007. It was a supposed fall through space that lasted for a while, it was nerve racking, and it made me think of the possibility of the outer darkness Jesus spoke to, the bottomless pit just falling through space forever.

As real as the simulated space fall felt to me, it gave me the idea that a bottomless pit exists.

On the other hand, the New Testament concept derived from the Greek term *πνεῦμα pneuma*, it is linked directly with the supernatural, defined in Strongs as Christ's Spirit or the Holy Spirit. Although some scholars use these two words *rûach* and *pneuma* interchangeably for both the human spirit and the Holy Spirit as the breath of God.

I, however, divorce the two concepts, one the creational concept at the time of our conception, *rûach* as our spirit given to each as the gift of life. The Greek word *pneuma*, I bring into context as the Holy Spirit, given to each as they are born again into the Kingdom of God.

The unification of the breath of life, and the Holy Spirit links up the triune human with the triune God, spirit communicating with spirit and in truth.

The *pneuma* period could also be classified as the baptism of the spirit with fire, as was proclaimed by John in Luke 3:16 (KJV)

"*John answered, saying unto them all, I indeed baptize you with water; but one mightier than I cometh, the latchet of whose shoes I am not worthy to unloose: he shall baptize you with the Holy Ghost and with fire".*

Thus, the order of the spirit is in two parts, the breath of God, *rûach*, the gift of life, then the re-birth gift of the spirit pneuma, the eternal life given by God through the Holy Spirit.

This leaves us with another Greek word G2315 *θεόπνευστος, theopneustos* pronounced *theh-op'-nyoo-stos (Strongs G2315) which literally means divinely breathed in, or an inspiration of God. This concept speaks of divine intervention, the breathing in of Godly inspiration through the Holy Spirit.*

This establishes a firm medium from God's spirit to our spirit through the inspiration of the triune God which will influence and change the soul, or our mind. To understand the working of the spirit one should be in one accord with what is spiritual. However, this probably leaves the reader with questions about the linkage between spirit, mind, and body, this I will discuss to bring it into context shortly.

The triune body has a hierarchy which is first spirit, then mind (soul) and then body. Many have argued about the home of the spirit, some argue that the spirit is in the blood, others retain it is in the mind and is the higher element above the ego.

My scientific and spiritual observation in this regard, purports that the spirit is the life-giving function and that the mind or brain is the soul, which causes feelings of the heart. Hence the spirit works with, and controls much of the conscience and even of the sub-conscious mind. By implication, the spirit is awake 24/7 even whilst the soul rests or dreams. This implies that the engine room and control centre of the body is the mind, biblically termed the soul.

Accordingly, when the brain dies, so does the soul but the spirit departs from the body to its predestination, paradise or to await the great throne judgement in a place commonly termed hades or hell, here I refer to John's revelation of the great throne judgement in Revelation 20:11- 15, I quote:

"And I saw a great white throne, and him that sat on it, from whose face the earth and the heaven fled away; and there was found no place for them. And I saw the dead, small and great, stand before God; and the books were opened: and another book was opened, which is the book of life: and the dead were judged out of those things which were written in the books, according to their works. And the sea gave up the dead which were in it; and death and hell delivered up the dead which were in them: and they were judged every man according to their works. And death and hell were cast into the lake of fire. This is the

second death. And whosoever was not found written in the book of life was cast into the lake of fire" (KJV).

Herewith I introduce the dynamics of a spiritual growth model based on 1Corintinthians 12 and utilizing Greek terminology to describe the specific stages as depicted in Figure 1 - Spiritual Growth model (Ferguson 2019a)

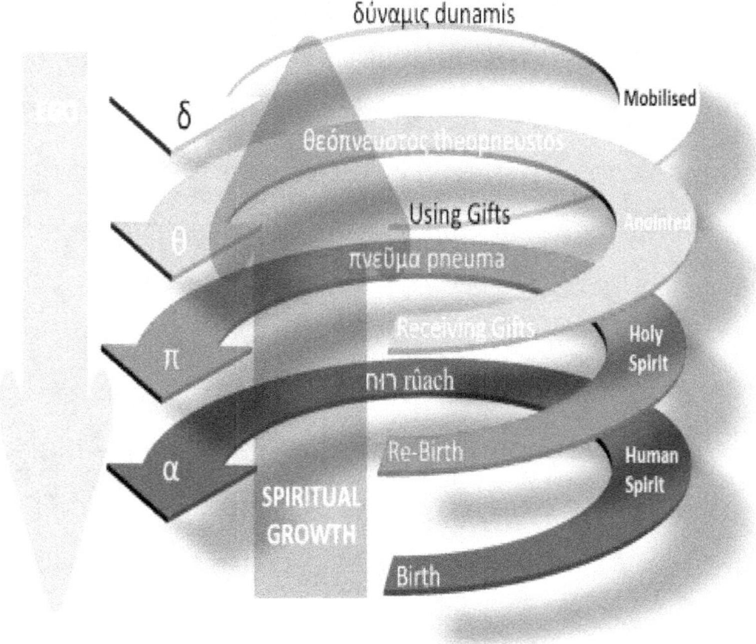

Figure 1 - Spiritual Growth model (Ferguson 2019a)

Because I have outlined the godly traits of the spirit, it presupposes that spiritual living as Paul puts it, will influence the way the mind interprets what is right, wrong, good, bad, or sinful.

Similarly, the Holy Spirit as pneuma acts on the rûach our living spirit which proceeding through the theopneustos phase, which is the Godly inspiration, or could even be classed as one's anointing. The matter that is of great concern is that the *theopneustos* phase is heavily dependent on spiritual activity, sanctification, humility, prayer and even fasting.

Hence, spiritual power is imparted by divine intervention through the Holy Spirit which is determined by the amount of spiritual capability a believer has to do the will of God by exercising the gifts of the spirit as listed by Paul in 1Corinthians 12:7-11 (KJV)

"*But the manifestation of the Spirit is given to every man to profit withal. For to one is given by the Spirit the word of wisdom; to another the word of knowledge by the same Spirit; To another faith by the same Spirit; to another the gifts of healing by the same Spirit; To another the working of miracles; to another prophecy; to another discerning of spirits; to another diverse kinds of tongues; to another the interpretation of tongues: But all these worketh that one and the self-same Spirit, dividing to every man severally as he will".*

Therefore, as Paul refers to manifestation of the nine listed gifts: wisdom, knowledge, faith, healing, miracles, discernment, speaking in unknown tongues, interpretation, and prophecy, I believe there are preconditions to the impartation of the gifts through the process theopneustos.

One should understand that the greatest threat to Lucifer's work is when a true believer enters the spiritual realm. When believers ignore the spiritual realm, the open wide the playing field of Satan and the demonic. Likewise, when the believer enters the spiritual realm clothed with the Greek term *δύναμις dunamis*, pronounced *doo'-nam-is* (Strongs G1411), a spiritually powerful state, enacted by the theopneustos stage, the demonic tremble and flee.

At this stage, the righteousness of God takes the centre stage giving way to miraculous works of the spirit. However, by implication the *dunamis* stage cannot take place prior to *theopneustos. It is because the theopneustos* causes a shift in the spiritual dimension that empowers the spiritual warrior, the gifted child of God.

Each of the nine gifts of the spirit empower the believer with weapons of insight and intervention from God through our Spirit to the physical, visible, and audible dimension that will at times go beyond any scientific rule or theory.

Therefore, the four stages of spiritual empowerment stem from God, yet these are not open to everyone, only those who are prepared to move from stage one through to four. One is saddened by the fact that there are so few Christians that understand or endeavour to reach stage four. This would be where they could optimally utilise their gifts of the Spirit.

Notably, the advantage of the gifts of the spirit are shunned by certain sectors of the church terming such activity as unorderly.

When the working of the spirit is subdued by the leadership of the Church, it puts the church member at a spiritual disadvantage. However, bold spiritual leaders allow the orderly advancement and use of the gifts of the spirit in the church by ensuring such are genuine.

Therefore, by implication, each of the gifts of the spirit reveal the truth of the Word (Jesus), which is concluded by the Holy Spirit. Hence, the gifts of the spirit are revelatory to the past present and future and annul the plans and tactics of Satan.

Nonetheless, one should understand that taking away the gifts of the spirit from the church, is likened to church members placing all spiritual weaponry in storage, reducing spiritual security to nil.

It is careless of spiritual leaders to condemn the gifts of the spirit or even to label them for specialised use only. These are part and parcel of a believer's outfit to allow for spiritual capability and security. I will discuss the matter in more detail in the chapter on spiritual warfare.

Once one understands that the omnipresence and omnipotence of God is proclaimed by the Holy Spirit, and the more we interact with God in this way, the easier it becomes to personalise the relationship with God through prayer. When a believer calls on God, several processes take place which I shall list and discuss so that the concept of the Holy Spirit and prayer can be taken on by the reader.

Unpacking the Gifts of the Holy Spirit

I shift my focus from the bottom two layers of my spiritual growth model Figure 1 - Spiritual Growth model (Ferguson 2019a) by recapping that dunamis stage cannot take place prior to the theopneustos state. In the theopneustos state one receives the gifts as a decisive impartation from God, through the Holy Spirit. The dunamis state is where the believer acts out his/her gifts.

Unfortunately, so many never reach the dunamis level because they are discouraged to exercise their gifts or are not bold enough to do the work of the spirit. In my observation of the church of about 50 plus years, God used those who were bold enough to take up their gifts and they could use them from the kitchen to their workplace, from the hospitals to the church. The most fascinating phenomenon about the dunamis stage is that when the Spirit of God has the supreme authority in a person, the dynamic power of God causes change in various ways that often surprise even the gifted believer. Therefore, to unpack the gifts of the spirit of Corinthians 12:8-11 see Figure 2 - Gifts of the Spirit (Ferguson 2019b)

In the unpacking process I shall attempt to shed light on each of the gifts in three ways: one the definition; two, it is uses in the theopneustos state and three, the dynamics of the gift in the dunamis state. The purpose of this discussion is to empower the reader with the necessary knowledge required to put his / her gifts to work.

A word of warning though, the balance of humility and the authority in Christ is key, once the work of the Holy Spirit is taken over by the instrument (the gifted believer) the sincerity of the operation is diluted, and the ego of the instrument gets in the way. Thus, with my warning in mind, one treads carefully through the acceptance of the gifts knowing that they are not there to satisfy the human ego or to bring popularity to the instrument being used by God. Unfortunately, many a once humble servant of God, has fallen into the ego trap which Satan sets up and supports very well.

I shall proceed with the unpacking of the gifts of the Spirit. I again stress the fact that the *dunamis* stage cannot be entered successfully without much prayer and even fasting.

Figure 2 - Gifts of the Spirit (Ferguson 2019b)

The Gift of Prophecy

I start at the centre of the circle with **prophecy** - it is defined by David Guzik,(10)wherein he relates to prophecy: "*in the Biblical understanding, isn't necessarily 'fore-telling' in a strictly predictive sense. It is more accurately 'forth-telling' the heart and mind of God, which may or may not include a predictive aspect*".

Yet Guzik further to warns believers against "*flippant, 'stream of consciousness' prophecy that has no difficulty saying, 'Thus says the Lord' at the drop of a hat*". I too share his sentiment about what I call 'ego prophecy' where so called prophets prophecy in the name of the Lord whilst their prophetic word is empty and in cases become self-fulfilling, and which were never from God in the first place.

Let us start with the truth about the gift of prophecy, it cannot be handed over to someone unless ordained by God himself, secondly, the gift as any other cannot be taught, only we can teach about how to use the gift, if a person does not have the gift, they cannot make it up or 'fake it till they make it', even though many have tried. It is almost like someone wanting to be an opera vocalist when the candidate has a squeaky voice with little or no vocal giftedness whatsoever.

Whilst I believe in the gift of prophecy, and I listen to prophetic word handed down by prophets, I do test prophecy in three ways. Firstly, is the prophecy relevant to the past, present or future? Secondly, if the prophecy is from God, how is it backed up by two or three ordinances: Scripture, a Word of truth and / or another prophecy? Last, but not least, how did God speak to the individual being prophesied to in his/her mind or heart about the matter.

Therefore, as Paul did, I encourage believers to prophecy if they have the gift, if they do not, they should refrain from tarnishing it, by trying to use great spiritual weaponry without having the heavenly license to do so.

Now then the question may arise, how does one know if one has the gift of prophecy? Back to the theopneustos state, such a gift will be revealed by the master, the Holy Spirit. Prophetic words will manifest, one may give a word of warning to someone and the warning and its consequence came to pass. In another case God may reveal a matter to one about someone else, or their situation. When one acts in obedience, it may be that a prophetic word is given to the person in question, and a proclamation for a solution to the problem is rendered. In other cases, prophets see visions or dream dreams that have meaning, Daniel and John are good examples of prophetic revelation through visions. Thus, prophecy should and is part and parcel of spiritual weaponry that is so very important to the church as it reveals the heart of God for the present and the future.

Prophecy in the dunamis state is so powerful that it will confront sin or unrighteousness, speak to the cause of a problem, and will propose a solution or a consequence for disobedience. True prophecy is powerful and will not be people pleasing and will not be classed as Christian fortune telling in any way.

The Gift of Healing

The gift of healing is mentioned three consecutive times by Paul in 1Corinthians 12:9, 28 and 30, however, Jesus, speaking to the disciples on the great commission in Mark 16:16 to 18 puts several gifts at the forefront. The gifts Jesus specifies are driving out devils, speaking in new tongues, being protected from deadly incidents, and laying hands on the sick for them to recover. I quote Mark 16:16-18 for the ease of the reader (KJV)

"*He that believeth and is baptized shall be saved; but he that believeth not shall be damned. And these signs shall follow them that believe; In my name shall they cast out devils; they shall speak with new tongues; They shall take up serpents; and if they drink any deadly thing, it shall not hurt them; they shall lay hands on the sick, and they shall recover*".

Consequently, the gift of healing is referred to by Guzik[(10)]as "God's healing power, either *given* or *received*, and has been repeatedly documented in the New Testament and since". Thus, I refer to the documented healings that took place in the Gospels and the later in the book of

Acts. Healing has become a very significant part of evangelisation where these have been documented through the ages.

Within the context of healings, it seems to be a gift that believers have immediately after being baptized. Therefore, whilst Paul lists the gift under the gifts of the Holy Spirit, one must concede that the gift of healing seems to come with baptism, and it is implied that believers have the power to pray for the sick and they will be healed. Thus, this gift is available in three stages *pneuma, theopneustos* and *dunamis*.

One sees that this gift is given together with others in Mark 16:16-18, at the baptism of the believer. In conclusion the gift of healing for the healing of the believer's body and can come through prayer by the laying on of hands, holy communion and or where two or three gather in Jesus' name to pray for the sick.

The Gift of Discernment

Simpson & Weiner[11] define the meaning of the noun discernment as "to judge well" although in the Biblical contect this is also true, discernment has a more richer meaning in the theopneustos and dunamis stage.

It encompasses the determination of God's view on situations and will be linked to discerning of good versus evil as well as the knowledge of the presence of the demonic. Furthermore, the gift of discernment will even judge a person or group's attitude in the spiritual realm. This gift comes with responsibility of note and not everyone has it although many would love to engage life with it.

Discernment in the Bible goes way back and started with Jacob when he discerned that his wife had stolen her father's idols. The people in the Bible who had the gift of discernment to a greater of lesser extent were Jacob, Joseph, Samuel, David, Solomon, Elijah, Elisha, Daniel and probably every other known prophet in the Old Testament.

In the New Testament Jesus, Peter, Paul, Apollos, John, and others. The gift bodes well with, but is not limited to, the calling of the prophet and the apostle.

The gift of discernment can be compared with a feeling about a matter, good or bad and in certain cases the feeling comes as a warning. Discernment has to do with past, present, and future and encompasses the insight to the will of God in a matter. On the other hand, this gift may provide insight into demonic or Angelic activity. Therefore, the person that discerns does so under the guidance of the Holy Spirit and would require practicing the use of such, to deal with what is revealed to him/her in the most appropriate manner.

Notwithstanding the previous discussion, discernment comes with a responsibility to act, to wait, or to speak out. Thus, discernment has three purposes, one to diagnose or test, the other to make sound judgment and lastly to conclude in an action, whether passive or active.

The acting out of discernment can be by means of a word of warning about the here and now with a future consequence. Or it could be a command to the demonic to leave a person or an area, and it may be that the discerning act leaves the discerner with certain knowledge that would be key information required to solve a matter or even a mystery. As the gifts are unpacked one finds the linkage from one to another with one common purpose, to empower the body of Christ.

The author of Hebrews writes in Chapter 5:12-14 (KJV)

"For when for the time ye ought to be teachers, ye have need that one teach you again which be the first principles of the oracles of God; and are become such as have need of milk, and not of strong meat. For everyone that useth milk is unskillful in the word of righteousness: for he is a babe. But strong meat belongeth to them that are of full age, even those who by reason of use have their senses exercised to discern both good and evil".

This passage of scripture emphasizes the maturity of the person who administers the gift within God's kingdom. Hence, one may conclude that discernment comes with spiritual maturity.

The Gift of Miracles

Defining a miracle is based Ransom & Alicke(12)in their study on lay minister's belief in miracles, show that people view miracles as being events that are highly improbable and that such will instill faith in people as these become spiritually beneficial. In my view miracles are such events that defy the laws of science, the root of impossibility that is made possible by a spiritual breakthrough. Albeit the gift of miracles stems from Jesus' teaching preceding the Lord's prayer in Mark 11:22-24 (KJV). I quote

"*And Jesus answering saith unto them, Have faith in God. For verily I say unto you, that whosoever shall say unto this mountain, Be thou removed, and be thou cast into the sea; and shall not doubt in his heart but shall believe that those things which he saith shall come to pass; he shall have whatsoever he saith. Therefore, I say unto you, what things soever ye desire, when ye pray, believe that ye receive them, and ye shall have them*".

However, one should never misplace miracles or the gift, as it is the journey of making impossibilities becoming real. A miracle may be so big that is visible to a thousand people, yet it can be so small that only one knows about it. Yet, the small miracle is as good as the big mountain that moved. One should understand how Jesus did miracles, he calmed a storm recorded in Mark 4:38-40 and Luke 8:23-25, he told the wind to be still and the sea to be calm, and it was so. Another miracle he was prepared to share with Peter in Mathew 14:27-31, Jesus was walking on the water and invited Peter to do so to, Peter did until his faith failed him. Thus, miracles are linked to faith and vice versa. It seems like faith and miracle go hand in glove, without the one the other cannot happen, I truly believe that miracles happen all around us every day and that often we only see the big ones and forget the small.

The gift of miracles working in the in the theopneustos and dunamis stage bring meaning to making the impossible happen. A word spoken can break drought, make an eye grow in an empty socket and bring one a solution out of nowhere. In 1994, I was praying one morning, after prayer, I left the house through my lounge door that had an automatic lock on it, it closed behind me the I realised I had locked myself out and all the keys were in the house.

The house was extremely well secured; however, I remembered a schoolboy trick as a solution to my problem. If I would insert newspaper under the kitchen door, tap the key out from the outside, it would fall on the paper on the inside of the kitchen floor, and I could pull out the key from under the door.

I tried, all went according to plan until I pushed the key too hard from the outside of the door, I heard it cling on the floor off the paper and looking under the door, no key on the paper. I was very upset, almost in rage, I jerked the newspaper out from under the door with speed and tossed it on the side of the swimming pool behind me. It was then, I knew that I would have to find tools to break the hinges of the door.

Yet, in this moment of unhappiness, I said out loud "Lord, I have just prayed, believing that you would bless my day, and now this. I need a miracle, as I cannot get into the house at all". Albeit a moment later, I turned around to where I had thrown the newspaper, lo and behold, the newspaper was open wide and plum centre, as if someone had put it there, in the crease of the paper, I saw the kitchen key that I had bumped out on the floor. The key was picked up off the floor and put on the paper for me, this was real, not magic, a real miracle.

To summarise the gift of miracles, I would posit that this gift is within reach of any believer who has faith in God, that God can move mountains. Practice makes perfect, miracles come to fruition when we are in dire need of a solution, or when a group of people are in trouble. This is the best time to practice and believe in miracles: they come in many sizes, magnitude, and variances. Remember this one thing, God does the miracle, we speak and believe in it.

The Gift of Wisdom

Charles(13)poses the question to children, "Why do you think this request pleased God?" He posits that what pleased God was that Solomon's request for wisdom was not self-centered. I start with this because one will equate wisdom with Solomon, yet to have the gift of wisdom one should take the approach of being God centered first. Wisdom is truly from God and brings with it many keys to unlock spiritual and carnal treasure storehouses.

Therefore, I would like to quote Solomon's meeting with God in 2Chronicles 1:10-12(KJV)

"*Give me now wisdom and knowledge, that I may go out and come in before this people: for who can judge this thy people, that is so great? And God said to Solomon, Because this was in thine heart, and thou hast not asked riches, wealth, or honour, nor the life of thine enemies, neither yet hast asked long life; but hast asked wisdom and knowledge for thyself, that thou mayest judge my people, over whom I have made thee king: Wisdom and knowledge is granted unto thee; and I will give thee riches, and wealth, and honour, such as none of the kings have had that have been before thee, neither shall there any after thee have the like*".

The miracle that happened here is that knowledge, which is a cognitive attribute to implement wisdom, was given to Solomon at the same time.

This is astounding because Solomon was not taught at a university, neither does the Bible relate to his education as a boy. He was impregnated with the astounding knowledge that God gave him so that he would judge well, when called upon to do so. It is prudent to realise that God favoured Solomon because of his selfless attitude as a young boy. This goes to say that the gift of wisdom should be utilised in selflessness to ensure that it is used for the good of the body of Christ and not for individuals or special groups.

Yang[14] Defines wisdom as "*a real-life process which consists of three core components—integration, embodiment, and positive effects*". Although his study proves to include all three I propose to add a fourth which is a spiritual insight, which is the area which not all will be privileged to experience, this is for those who live by the spirit as explained by Paul in 1Corinthians 2:9-12 (KJV) and I quote

"*But as it is written, Eye hath not seen, nor ear heard, neither have entered into the heart of man, the things which God hath prepared for them that love him. But God hath revealed them unto us by his Spirit: for the Spirit searcheth all things, yea, the deep things of God. For what man knoweth the things of a man, save the spirit of man which is in him? even so the things of God knoweth no man, but the Spirit of God. Now we have received, not the spirit of the world, but the spirit which is of God; that we might know the things that are freely given to us of God*".

Accordingly, we have a privilege to utilise and be contained in Godly wisdom when we judge in the dunamis stage. One needs to know that we have access to a source of Godly wisdom not by our own doing, but by the Holy Spirit who works in and around us. As in the case of Daniel in so many Old Testament stories, carnal wisdom is outrun by the eternal wisdom of God given to us through the Holy Spirit.

If ever there was a time that wisdom is required, it is to fathom the COVID-19 global pandemic that has plagued the world with infections increasing at an alarming ratio of about one person infecting three others. This unexpected pandemic has brought the world to a standstill and literally and figuratively, the church to its knees. The flooding of the church with apocalyptic information, facts, fallacy and so many different assumptions makes interpretation and evaluation of the disease, and relevance to the Church and the end times, rather difficult.

In this case Church leaders require wisdom to guide and navigate their congregants through the storm. In closing on the gift of wisdom, it is supernatural wisdom that allows one to have Godly insights into earthly matters, this may include prophetic insight, visionary thinking, and solutions to big and small problems.

The Gift of Knowledge

One should start out with where Knowledge was first mentioned in the Bible, in Genesis 2:9 (KJV) and I quote,

"And out of the ground made the LORD God to grow every tree that is pleasant to the sight, and good for food; the tree of life

also in the midst of the garden, and the tree of knowledge of good and evil".

Knowledge was one of the first attributes which allowed the human being to distinguish between right and wrong. Although it came through disobedience, it has remained the life-long companion of the human being.

Thus, as knowledge is dependent on intelligence, and gaining it increases the level of the intellect.

Yet God allowed intellect to build inside humans, in their DNA, over thousands of years, so much so that same creation, the human, is questioning its maker, God. One needs to appreciate that God is the father of creation and the owner of its entire knowledge base. Albeit, the human has always had a quest to gain more knowledge about the creation, sources of energy, the breath of life and even the reason for living by virtue of his/her philosophies.

Furthermore, the human mind has a quest for finding the origin of life, the earth, nature and as much as the furthermost parts of the universe. The knowledge of human account is as far and as good as the investigative instruments that evolve for him/her.

At the same time, the human is inclined to look for God however his/her knowledge somehow gets in the way of their spiritual understanding. Herewith I proclaim the difference between gained knowledge and revealed knowledge.

Once one taps into the source of all knowledge, God, in fact one can take it further, to John 1: 1-3 (GNB) and I quote

"In the beginning the Word already existed; the Word was with God, and the Word was God. From the very beginning the Word

was with God. Through him God made all things; not one thing in all creation was made without him. The Word was the source of life, and this life brought light to people".

This light is the knowledge of God, the kind that supersedes that knowhow gained through scientific means. Thus, the knowledge acquired from God contains the revelation of light. It seeks to delight God, to open and to reveal the truth of a moment or even of many years into the future.

The gift of knowledge is one that will take the Word of Truth, bring the light of God onto, or even into situations. This knowledge is spiritual and reveals and unravels mysteries of God, revealing the knowledge given to us through scripture, relating such to life and to the realities believers face daily. Finally, the gift of knowledge is a very important gift and will ensure that the truth of God could be shared with the believers, in testimony of the will of God or even needed revelation.

The Gift of Speaking in Other Tongues

Unfortunately speaking in tongues is not for the faint hearted, the unbeliever or the critic. It just will not happen to them, or if it does, God wants to prove a point to them. What one can say is that the first sign after the wind in the upper-room and tongues of fire, was that everyone in the room was speaking in in unknown tongue to the one they spoke. I refer to Acts 2:1 to 8 (KJV)

"And when the day of Pentecost was fully come, they were all with one accord in one place. And suddenly there came a sound from heaven as of a rushing mighty wind, and it filled all the house where they were sitting. And there appeared unto them

cloven tongues like as of fire, and it sat upon each of them. And they were all filled with the Holy Ghost, and began to speak with other tongues, as the Spirit gave them utterance. And there were dwelling at Jerusalem Jews, devout men, out of every nation under heaven. Now when this was noised abroad, the multitude came together, and were confounded, because that every man heard them speak in his own language. And they were all amazed and marvelled, saying one to another, Behold, are not all these which speak Galileans? And now hear we every man in our own tongue, wherein we were born?".

Yet the Gospel of Mark speaks to the speaking in tongues at the Great Commission, in Mark 16: 17 (KJV)

"And these signs shall follow them that believe; In my name shall they cast out devils; they shall speak with new tongues". Then throughout Acts one sees that

speaking in other tongues "languages" remained prevalent, Acts 2:3,4, 2:11, 10:46, 19:6. It seemed to be part and parcel of the service. Also, Holy Spirit visitations were very prevalent bringing about miracles and wonders throughout the book of Acts, written by Luke between 60 and 90A.D. meaning about at least 40 years of the early church was captured in this book of the New Testament. By implication, the early Church was used to the gifts of the spirit, the works of the Holy Spirit and what we would probably call evangelical revival today.

Consequently, Paul's explanation about speaking in tongues, 1 Corinthians, coincides with as many questions about the matter as we have today. Notably, with the church of Acts it was about a 30 plus year journey, bringing the Holy Spirit and tongues to the Gentile world, Greece, Italy, North Africa, Spain, actually, the entire Roman

Grecian world in AD 32 to AD 90 and after. Also read about tongues in 1 Corinthians 12, 13 & 14. This is almost the only place, other than Acts where the speaking in tongues is prominent. Thus, in summary, speaking in tongues is referenced in Mark, Acts and 1 Corinthians.

I will never be apologetic about speaking in tongues at all, as I always say, if you have experienced anything, it cannot be told that it does not exist or that it should not happen again. I was 11 years old when I first experienced the anointing of God through the Holy Spirit and by speaking in tongues. In our church it was something special, almost a must. Yet, what I found out even at that age was that the gift and sin do not mix. So here is a childlike story, that may clear up a thing or two in your mind, about God working through His Holy Spirit in men and woman who really seek his face.

My dad and mom would send me to the shop for bread daily, and at that time a loaf cost 11 cents. My dad would give me 12 cents, and I would short-change him and use the other cent for a sweet. This carried on for a while, then one day he gave me 15 cents, I bought a bigger sweet and while munching away, I walked out of the shop and my new bicycle was gone, it had been stolen. Well, this was a lesson on its own, I truly believed my bicycle was stolen because I stole from my dad.

That weekend, an evangelist was praying at church for people to be filled with the Holy Spirit and to speak in tongues. I stood in front with one conviction, the short-changing stood between me and God. I made a promise to God, that if he would baptize me with the Holy Spirit, and I speak in tongues, I will repent after church, which I did. The anointing of God came over me, do not know what I was saying, but I was speaking in other tongues.

Now, I take this one step further, when people start speaking in tongues for the first time, from my personal experience, maybe two or three words of a new vocabulary. Just as learning another language the vocabulary increases with practice. So too, as a person practices to speak the heavenly language, the vocabulary increases. Also, I was told by a missionary once working in the Congo, in the 1980's, he was in a service where people where speaking Afrikaans as a strange tongue, and he understood the language. On another occasion my mother, in the 1970's had spoken in tongues in a service, after the service a Greek lady came up to her and thanked her for the message, her words were, "thank you, you told me in my own language God loves me!". These statements are true, as true as speaking in tongues comes through the Holy Spirit and from God.

I close with the words of Paul in 1Corinthians 14:39-40 (KJV) "*Wherefore, brethren, covet to prophesy, and forbid not to speak with tongues. Let all things be done decently and in order*".

The Gift of Interpretation

The gift of interpretation goes as far back as Joseph in Genesis, the dream interpretation, the butler and the baker and others in Genesis 40 and 41. Also in Judges 7 with Gideon, and especially in the book of Daniel. Thus, the gift of interpretation may start with the interpretation of dreams.

Conversely, I caution that dream interpretation is a common practice of psychology and the New Age cult. Therefore, one should not be confusing a gift of the spirit with the unclean rituals and practices of eastern religion and even using their techniques of colour, animals, insects, creatures, plants, and the like. These are not based on Biblical principles and I encourage believers not to go and borrow techniques which dilute the work of the Holy Spirit. One should even condemn some Christian dream interpretation literature that is based on Eastern and African religion. On the other hand, some believers have the gift of interpreting dreams through the Holy Spirit and discernment. I have stumbled across a number of Christian writings that incorporate the works of secularist and new age teachers and as these infiltrates the Church, the lies of Satan are used as the truth of God, this is detrimental to the spiritual wellbeing of the believers.

However, in my next discussion I focus on the interpretation of tongues, and I refer to 1Corinthians 12:10 – 11 (KJV)

"*To another the working of miracles; to another prophecy; to another discerning of spirits; to another diverse kinds of tongues; to another the interpretation of tongues: But all these worketh that one and the selfsame Spirit, dividing to every man severally as he will*".

As is explained by Paul, the gift of interpretation works in tandem with the gift of speaking in tongues. One person may speak in tongues, bringing a message from God through the Holy Spirit in a divine moment, and another would interpret so that those in the congregation or audience may understand and be encouraged.

However, Paul, knowing the work of the Holy Spirit and understanding the liturgy of the service, explains in 1Corinthians 14:26-28 (KJV) "*How is it then, brethren? when ye come together, every one of you hath a psalm, hath a doctrine, hath a tongue, hath a revelation, hath an interpretation. Let all things be done unto edifying. If any man speaks in an unknown tongue, let it be by two, or at the most by three, and that by course; and let one interpret. But if there be no interpreter, let him keep silence in the church; and let him speak to himself, and to God".*

In my case I only received the gift of interpretation at the age of eighteen, although, I had received the gift of speaking in tongues at the age of eleven. When I interpret a message in tongues, I usually only get the first two to five words that I will start speaking with, after this the words just flow. However, the practicality of these gifts is, if one practices them, and one's heart is pure before God, the Holy Spirit can use such a person to encourage the congregation or even two or three in a group.

Some folks have asked if this could be a barometer of the spirituality and depth of prayer in a congregation, to this I answer, where God's Spirit is welcome, it is omnipresent and will use and speak through those who hear his voice. A clean and clear, sinless conscience allows one to enter the presence of God in such a way that one can interpret mysteries and tongues through the gifting of the Spirit. Unfortunately, sin may shut down the voice of the Holy Spirit, and unfortunately this is true about our post millennial church.

The Gift of faith

As I discuss the last gift, the one of faith, I believe we all have it because it is the basis on which we accept Christ as our personal saviour, I quote Romans 5:1-2 (KJV) "*Therefore being justified by faith, we have peace with God through our Lord Jesus Christ. By whom also we have access by faith into this grace wherein we stand and rejoice in hope of the glory of God*".

Nevertheless, there is a greater faith the Jesus speaks about in Mathew 17 and repeats it in Matthew 21:21-22 (KJV) and I quote,

"*Jesus answered and said unto them, Verily I say unto you, If ye have faith, and doubt not, ye shall not only do this which is done to the fig tree, but also if ye shall say unto this mountain, Be thou removed, and be thou cast into the sea; it shall be done. And all things, whatsoever ye shall ask in prayer, believing, ye shall receive*".

In the discussion on the gift of faith, one must understand it is an inherent kind of knowing or experience that God can and will answer a prayer, request or even a sigh. Our knowledge that God the Father understands everything about us, so much so that He numbers the hairs on our head is what grows faith. Therefore, as one's faith grows with this knowledge of God, it turns into a knowing that God will never let us down. Still there are times when one gets into a situation where unbelief makes us falter.

As faith grows into knowledge of God, the gift delivers miracles, and the mere spoken word of a believer into the spiritual realm can cause remarkable changes for whatever cause and by the will of God. Yet, as I wrote this book, I too realised that the entire unexposed power through prayer happens by faith which is a result of action. I quote James 2:26 (KJV)

"*For as the body without the spirit is dead, so faith without works is dead also*".

The exercise for Chapter 7 is divided into two specific areas, namely levels of prayer, see assignment on spiritual maturity and unpacking the gifts of the Spirit.

Assignment: – Spiritual Maturity

1. What are the four levels or areas of growth in spiritual maturity?

2. What happens to the human ego in the theopneustos or anointed state of one's prayer life

3. Why is it important for a believer to pray and act in the Dunamis or Mobilised state of prayer and faith.

4. Why is the anointing of God so important when praying in the spirit?

5. Do you think most believer's prayer lives operate in the theopneustos or dunamis state, and which is the most relevant to having spiritual authority?

Assignment: Gifts of the Spirit

1. List the nine gifts of the Spirit
2. Which of these gifts do you have?
3. Why is praying in tongues important?
4. How would you describe the gift of discernment?
5. Can the gift of prophecy be handed over by human teaching?
6. Should prophecy be tested and why?
7. Can one person have all nine gifts of the spirit? Was this intended to be so?
8. Which of the gifts which you do not have, do you desire?
9. Should the gifts of the Holy Spirit operate in the Church meetings or not and why?
10. Why is the gift of healing for the believer in relation to Mark 16:16 to 18?
11. In Mark 16:17 the believer is promised to speak in tongues, is this still relevant for our churches and why?
12. What power has the believer over the demonic and why?

13. Evaluating your use of the gifts, rate yourself 1 to 10 one lowest, ten highest
14. What do you need to do to up your score?

CHAPTER 7

Prayer and spiritual warfare

The power of prayer is not always understood as a means of making war in the spiritual realm. It is almost as if the believer is unaware of the spiritual world and its purpose. For the believer there is a definite line of defense and it starts with the Angelic, then one rank up the Holy Spirit, then Son and the Father.

The Father commands the Angelic and they fall under the command of Archangels, Michael, the head of angles of war, Gabriel the Guardian Angel, incidentally the only two Archangels spoken about in the Bible other than Lucifer, the archangel angel of death.

The Archangel, Michael's work is revealed in Daniel 10:11-12 (KJV) *The angel said to me,*

"Daniel, God loves you. Stand up and listen carefully to what I am going to say. I have been sent to you." When he had said this, I stood up, still trembling. Then he said, "Daniel, don't be afraid. God has heard your prayers ever since the first day you decided to humble yourself in order to gain understanding, I have come in answer to your prayer".

On the other hand, Gabriel as the messenger and the one who stands in the presence of God, also revealed in Daniel (Daniel 8 and 9) and again in Luke where he foretells the virgin birth and the birth of John the Baptist (Luke 1).

Lucifer too was in the highest rankings of heaven as the head of worship, he then tried to get control of the Angelic, this is recorded in *Isaiah 14:12-14* (KJV)

How you have fallen from heaven, morning star, son of the dawn! You have been cast down to the earth, you who once laid low the nations! You said in your heart, "I will ascend to the heavens; I will raise my throne above the stars of God; I will sit enthroned on the mount of assembly, on the utmost heights of the North. I will ascend above the tops of the clouds; I will make myself like the Most-High".

Yet another scripture speaks the God's intention in creating Lucifer versus his ultimate fall as God threw him out of heaven I quote a rather long passage for context Ezekiel 28:13-19 (KJV)

"*Thou hast been in Eden the garden of God; every precious stone* was *thy covering, the sardius, topaz, and the diamond, the beryl, the onyx, and the jasper, the sapphire, the emerald, and the carbuncle, and gold: the workmanship of thy tabrets and of thy pipes was prepared in thee in the day that thou wast created. Thou art the anointed cherub that covereth; and I have set thee so: thou wast upon the holy mountain of God; thou hast walked up and down in the midst of the stones of fire.*

Thou wast perfect in thy ways from the day that thou wast created, till iniquity was found in thee. By the multitude of thy merchandise, they have filled the midst of thee with violence, and thou hast sinned: therefore, I will cast thee as profane out of the mountain of God: and I will destroy thee, O covering cherub, from the midst of the stones of fire. Thine heart was lifted up because of thy beauty, thou hast corrupted thy wisdom by reason of thy brightness: I will cast thee to the ground, I will lay thee before kings, that they may behold thee. Thou hast defiled thy sanctuaries by the multitude of thine iniquities, by the iniquity of thy traffick; therefore, will I bring forth a fire from the midst of thee, it shall devour thee, and I will bring thee to ashes upon the earth in the sight of all them that behold thee. All they that know thee among the people shall be astonished at thee: thou shalt be a terror, and never shalt thou be any more".

In this I do not want to give any glory to Satan, but want to state, and empathically so, that he was created as a perfect Cherub, a being that could worship and sing, but when evil existed in him, he turned on God with a third of the then Angelic. God threw Satan out of heaven, not too much said about Lucifer in our Bible, because it is a handbook of the believer, and only what we need to know about him is written there.

We read of Lucifer as a deceiver as early as Genesis and it is with him our spiritual fight continues on earth. This is mostly because he tries to deceive and tempt us, also as he tried to tempt Jesus, the Son of God. Jesus shows his power over Satan and the demonic in about 40 different places in the four gospels, Matthew, Mark, Luke, and John.

These encounters one finds that Jesus drove out demons, even for the purpose of healing. Consequently, proving that the demonic can also manifest in sickness, disease and mental instability and the like.

Seventy-two disciples return from an evangelisation outreach that Jesus sent them on in Luke 10:17, they were excited about the miracles that happened through them. Jesus gives account to them and see how he says in in the first person, I quote Luke 10:18 (GNB)

"Jesus answered them, "I saw Satan fall like lightning from heaven".

That means Jesus was present when Satan was thrown out of heaven, and with a flash like lightning. Thereafter, Jesus gives them assurance that they have power over Satan and the demonic in, Luke 10:19 & 20 (GNB)

"Listen! I have given you authority, so that you can walk on snakes and scorpions and overcome all the power of the Enemy, and nothing will hurt you. But don't be glad because the evil spirits obey you; rather be glad because your names are written in heaven."

One should therefore not dismiss Jesus' cautionary comment that the most important is not that demons will obey the true believer, but that one's name is written in the book of life enabling eternal life. Jesus opens up a blessing in Luke 23 (b) and verse 24 (GNB),

"How fortunate you are to see the things you see! I tell you that many prophets and kings wanted to see what you see, but they could not, and to hear what you hear, but they did not".

In relation to this passage and its expose, there are two interpretations that come to the fore, one, that the privilege of having Jesus with them, and two, that they see with spiritual eyes what others before them have longed to see. Latching on to the discussion one can say, that having Jesus as a physical and spiritual mentor had opened-up the spiritual domain for them.

The Great Commission

Then the great commission given by Jesus to the disciples just before the ascension, Mark's version in Mark 16:17 & 18. It is so strange that the post millennial church does not encounter demons as Jesus or the disciples did, or are their spiritual eyes just closed? Surprisingly enough, where Jesus entered a place or region, the demonic cringed and made themselves known, Jesus knew them and drove them out. This was also the case with the New Testament disciples and Church. Is it the fear of Satan that holds the Church back from revealing the devil and his work, or does the work of the spirit not appeal to the church anymore?

In my opinion the Church has become a place of worship and not a place of spiritual activity, and if spiritual activity is allowed, it is so ordered that the devil knows where to find his gap.

Paul and Spiritual Warfare

So back to spiritual warfare then, does Paul does not say in 2Corinthians 10:3-5 (GNB)*"It is true that we live in the world, but we do not fight from worldly motives. The weapons we use in our fight are not the world's weapons but God's powerful weapons, which we use to destroy strongholds. We destroy false arguments; we pull down every proud obstacle that is raised against the knowledge of God; we take every thought captive and make it obey Christ"*. Our battle is not an earthy one and spiritual warfare should not be misconstrued with a silent prayer or two. Spiritual warfare is a combined battle in the spirit where the Angelic may also be involved. This kind of warfare is on a battlefield not seen or known to many, and if I may say, most believers because they have not been exposed to it or to the power of the battlefield. I purport that the spiritual battlefield is not for the faint hearted, or the faithless believer. To enter this warzone there are prerequisites, one, sinlessness, Satan will use your sin as an Achilles heel. Two, prayer and supplication, and three knowledge of God's word, if you quote it, it is a powerful weapon.

Spiritual warfare should never be misstated either, it has everything to do with the armoury of the spiritual warrior in Paul's letter to the Ephesians 6:13-15 *(GNB)*

"So put on God's armor now! Then when the evil day comes, you will be able to resist the enemy's attacks; and after fighting to the end, you will still hold your ground. So, stand ready, with truth as a belt tight around your waist, with righteousness as your breastplate, and as your shoes the readiness to announce the Good News of peace. At all times carry faith as a shield; for with it you will be able to put out all the burning arrows shot by the Evil One. And

accept salvation as a helmet, and the word of God as the sword which the Spirit gives you. Do all this in prayer, asking for God's help. Pray on every occasion, as the Spirit leads. For this reason, keep alert and never give up; pray always for all God's people".

Paul uses the analogy of a Roman soldier dressed for war because the civilisation of that time were aware of the military presence of the Romans in each town and city. So too we should be as vigilant about the omnipresence of our spiritual surroundings of principalities of darkness and the works of the spirit though the authority we have in Christ and by the Holy Spirit, omnipresent too and supposed to be living inside the believer. Thus, the aura of God's spirit should reside, and accompany believers in the rooms and places they visit, as ambassadors of heaven. Believers should walk and talk with spiritual authority, to anything and everything that tries to make them fail in their heavenly objectives.

Armoury of the Spirit

Paul breaks up the armoury of the spirit into truth, righteousness, readiness, faith, salvation, the word of God, and prayer, seven powerful weapons that will break down the strongholds around one. Hence, we should build a scenario so that the battlefield can be well understood. I list the three main areas namely 1) The Authority of Christ, his blood and the atonement at the right hand of the Father, 2) the Holy Spirit, 3) The Angelic 4) the believer's prayer and action, 5) the dominion of darkness and 6) the facet or problem of the believer in question. The unseen battle rages in the spiritual realm with the ultimate goal of freeing the believer of any danger.

However, the dominion of darkness deceives, lies, and does smoke and mirrors, to ensure that the believer does not find or see the solution of the problem, disease, or failure. God has already proclaimed the solutions before the believer even asks. One must remember that 99% of problems do have solutions, the order of darkness is likened to stinking wild dogs or hyenas, they always come in a pack and to irritate their prey when they feel helpless.

In the analogy, I propose that one sees that the problem is made much bigger by the howling in the mind by constant reminders of the problem that seems to have no solution or end. This could range from marital problems, personal, sickness, finances, work relations, unemployment family issues and as one probably knows, more than one of these problems seem to hit a person at once.

One needs to understand that Satan has the power to influence people. He also creates problems out of situations, then steers emotions and people to make wrong decisions, especially against God's will. He does this through temptation and deception. These wrong decisions of others, cause grief and emotional stress on the believer.

Perhaps, allow me to explain a scenario of a hijacking event: nothing is from God, it is Satan's work in other people, yet the hijacking of a believer, although protected by angels, is a mind-blowing traumatic event, caused by Satan's disciples.

The way Satan attacks

The way to attack an active believer is to use people, situations, and one's body to create problems for the believer. I have addressed the people part, now let us look at the situation facet of attack. This attack will be centered around the emotions and the messages of the situation will be heard, seen, tasted, or smelt. The sense of danger, or of the problem will race through the mind seeking a means to deny, approve, disapprove, or flee from it.

Yet, the reaction on the spiritual battlefield will be projected at a deterring the danger formed against the individual, and this comes through the discernment of the Holy Spirit echoing the scripture "greater is He that is in me, than He that is in the world".

Problems, however, can be categorised as follows, and the warfare will be different for each. One, immediate or short term: many times an emergency, two, problems that can be solved but need time and solutions, three, ones that are caused by or are health issues, four, those that ride emotions such as relationships, family, and marriage, five, those that can only be solved by miraculous intervention.

Back to the battlefield, here we have a raging war on believers. It is a 24/7 activity of the enemy to hound and cause situations that could break the faith of the believer. On the other side the protection is available by the authority of the name of and blood of Christ, by the Holy Spirit and then by the command of God the Father on the Angelic. The only way a believer can enter this battleground is through prayer and scripture confirmed by faith.

More prayer, more faith, more firing power. When the believer enters the battlefield the orders of darkness flee like burglars when the lights are suddenly switched on. Furthermore, whilst the believer cannot pray 24/7, the spiritual security is in place to ensure that no harm comes his/her way. This leads me to the importance of intercession.

The Intercessor

Let us first define an intercessor, because these individuals are often misused by other Christians who are too lazy to pray, who shift their responsibility onto someone else. An intercessor is a person who stands in the gap for others whilst they are at rest or unable to pray. These dear believers will pray purposefully for those in need of solutions and who often cannot enter the spiritual battlefield due to their circumstances, health, or the like.

The intercessor takes on the battle for another, even if the person or persons are not believers. However, the intercessory spans over many domains, including the most important, the saving of lost souls.

Ultimately then, one needs to picture the intercessor as someone who has been trained for war, will form a community of warriors, and who takes the strength in numbers to the battleground. This give expression to Jesus' words in Matthew 18:18-20 (GNB*)*

"And so I tell all of you: what you prohibit on earth will be prohibited in heaven, and what you permit on earth will be permitted in heaven. "And I tell you more: whenever two of you on earth agree about anything you pray for; it will be done for you by my Father in heaven. For where two or three come together in my name, I am there with them".

To not repeat myself again, may I remind the reader that the armoury and uniform of the intercessor are well explained in Ephesians 6 as previously outlined. Latching onto Jesus' words that where intercessors agree on earth on a matter, it will be so in heaven, which leads one to discover the real 24/7 intercessor, the Holy Spirit.

One must understand that whilst the believer intercedes there is action in heaven, and even more movement in the spiritual realm on earth. The Holy Spirit as Jesus foretold in John 16:13 (GNB)

"When, however, the Spirit comes, who reveals the truth about God, he will lead you into all the truth. He will not speak on his own authority, but he will speak of what he hears and will tell you of things to come".

Without labouring the point, one should understand that our spirit has the ability and capability to intercede through the Holy Spirit for ourselves and others not only through our conscious but also through our subconscious mind. That means even our mind, if not portioned with sin, can be unveiled unconsciously in the heavenlies through intercession without interception of any kind, I refer here to Satan and the demonic.

Therefore, the exposition of prayer goes far beyond the cognitive experience, the conscious and subconscious mind, and the mere spirit of mortal man. Prayer is the most powerful tool that God left with the human being for direct communication with Him, as the creator and ultimate Father of those born into the kingdom of Christ.

The Holy Spirit, living inside of us is always in communion with God the Father and the Son. The dimensions of spiritual value are indicative to the amount of time the believer spends in communion with God, through and by the Holy Spirit, the spirit of truth.

Music and the battlefield

The battle cry, because Satan understands music, and was created for it, hates the sound of the believer's praise and worship.

Thus, setting the tone on the battlefield one cannot ignore the power of Holy Spirit filled music, it levels the battleground as it sets the tone for God's glory.

Entering the battle with confirming music and a battle-cry of praise ensure that the presence and holiness of God defies the onslaught and influence of the demonic on the situation or war at hand.

What believers forget about the spiritual battleground is, that the battles that are won, are those where God and his will have been put first. There have been many lost battles where people have lost because they had put their own desires before the will of God. I quote Jesus' words in John 15:7 (GNB)

"If you remain in me and my words remain in you, then you will ask for anything you wish, and you shall have it".

The danger of the battleground is that Satan and the demonic do not level the playing-field and will do anything dark and disorderly to break the faith of the believer. They are terrorists and work on horror and terror of the body and mind of innocent victims. Thus, whilst the believer is strong the devil will cause division in families, relationships and try to break marital bonds to weaken the intercessor. The demonic will go for the weakest of the family, cause them harm to get back at the intercessor. Evil has no rules, limits, or boundaries, it is the Angelic and the Holy Spirit that puts up these barriers to protect the believer.

Therefore, here the battlefield moves from spiritual to carnal, the devil seeks to destroy those who are weak in faith so that the house can be divided. This has been the war tactic going back to centuries before Christ, the wars won are those that affected women and children at home, causing men to give up and surrender.

As intercessor you will need to place boundaries around your household, family, and friends in the spirit so that you control the movement of Satan and the demonic. Forgetting this, brings about casualties of war, your war, and your casualties. You will spend so much time and money mopping up, that there will be no time for intercessory prayer anymore.

In summary never enter the intercessory battlefield unprepared, without the armour you require or by yourself without the authority of Christ. I remind you of the words of an Angel to Zerubbabel in Zechariah 4:6 (GNB)

"The angel told me to give Zerubbabel this message from the LORD: "You will succeed, not by military might or by your own strength, but by my spirit".

Therefore, I propose, the battlefield is for a soldier who comes with the authority of the kingdom, in the uniform of Christ and with the spiritual armoury of heaven, with prayer as his/her vehicle for battle.

So many people enter the spiritual battlefield unprepared, they get injured and, in some cases, even their families and marriages do. I have set up a table of tasks for you to get prepared for the spiritual battlefield see the assignment on Spiritual Warfare. When you do war, you need to plan, simulate and strategies. Notably, spiritual warfare is no game, it serious and you need to prepare well before entering the battle zone in the Spirit. The armament the Holy Spirit brings is most important.

Assignment – Spiritual Warfare

1. Attack is the best means of defense; how will you approach such attacks in the spiritual territory and why?
2. When fear takes control of a situation, how would you exit it and how would you use scripture to bring certainty and faith back for the solution?
3. How and why would one be extremely careful of one's marriage and family bonds on the spiritual battlefield?
4. How would you unpack and inspect the spiritual armoury before going to battle?
5. What are your weaknesses? These will be exposed on the battlefield if you do not face them now.
6. Going into spiritual battle to win, with Satan who knows no rules, and who deceives, how do you face the unknown in the Spirit with the guidance of the Holy Spirit.

7. When injured on the battlefield, who will you call? Who and why would this person be trusted with your battle and your spiritual injury?
8. When celebrating victory, after winning a spiritual battle, how do you propose to stay humble so that you can maintain authority on the battlefield.
9. Describe how you would lead a team of prayer warriors, and what precautions should be in place?
10. Which family members should I cover with intercession for my own good?

CHAPTER 8 - Unanswered prayer

A believer is often confronted with unanswered prayer, and this is not uncommon at all. To answer this question is not easy when one's faith is so strong, backed up by Jesus' words in John 16:23-24 (GNB) "*When that day comes, you will not ask me for anything. I am telling you the truth: the Father will give you whatever you ask of him in my name. Until now you have not asked for anything in my name; ask and you will receive, so that your happiness may be complete*".

What is it then that stops prayers from being answered, this I intend unpacking because believers lose their objectivity, and often faith when they ask of God, and do not receive what they prayed for? Several topics come to mind as causes of unanswered prayer, these I list so that the phenomena are discussed in more detail:

1. God's will or not?
2. Does sin stand in the way of the answer?
3. Was the intended answer to the prayer for personal glory or for God's?
4. Does God intend answering the prayer later?
5. Does God not see my faith?
6. Does the faith of the person I am praying for affect the answer?
7. Does God put the prayers of others before mine?

God's will or not?

This is probably the most difficult question to answer as an author as God's will is different for everyone. One tries to fathom God's plan that not only spans earth, humanity, and the animal kingdom, but the entire universe. His grace does not limit his pan to the macro universe, but it is broken down into the microcosm of a single human being, you, and me. If God cares about the number of hairs on one's head, then surely His will on our lives is equally important.

Therefore, I begin to answer this question with a question. If a child asks to play with, or experiment with something that could cause a catastrophe, would it be wise for the parent to allow it? Most definitely not, no parent wants his \ her children to do anything that would endanger their wellbeing or their surroundings. The same applies to the will of God, if you ask for stupid things that will put you in danger, God may stop you in your tracks, do not be surprised by this.

Conversely, there is another aspect to God's will, and this is the bigger picture that goes unexplained as only God has it or knows it. Thus, fitting into God's bigger picture is part of the unknown plan. A good example are the early church martyrs: Peter and Paul, both imprisoned and executed. In their entire ministry they sought God's will, yet Paul was beheaded, and Peter crucified upside down. Were they outside of God's will to have earned death? Surely not, they were the foundation stone of the Church, laid next to their cornerstone, Jesus Christ, also crucified by God's will for salvation of humankind.

The will of God spirals up from his love for the individual, to family and through society, our country, the world, the universe and ultimately His eternal plan.

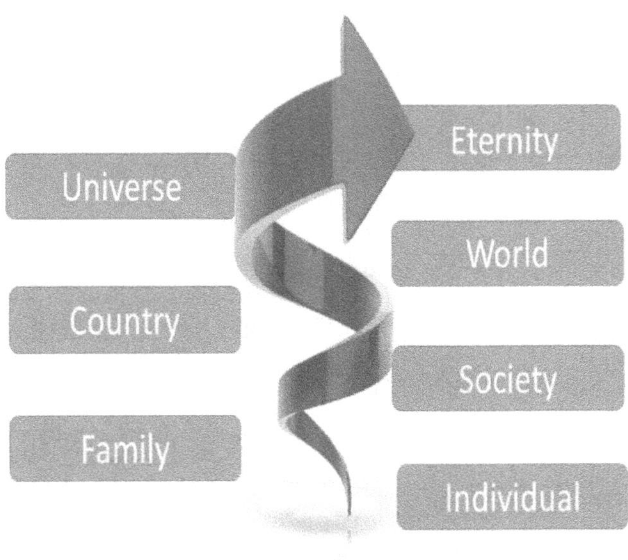

Figure 3- The upward spiral of God's will

Nevertheless, the supreme will of God then spirals up from the individual plan up and out through his eternal one. God's will shall surely be predominantly inclined to his majestic plan for the blue planet earth and the entire universe that includes the individual in the kingdom of God, which spans the entire world we live in. Therefore, seeking God's will, in our earthly context, will be impossible to gauge if this is not done through walking and talking with God.

Therefore, any communication barrier between the individual and God will ultimately hamper the knowledge one has of the will of God. Getting back to the early Church martyr I used in my analogy, one finds these children of God, living in his will, also died and paid a price within God's will and plan for the Church and kingdom of Christ.

The dearest lesson we have about the will of God and his love within it was the sacrifice of His Son on Calvary so that we would not have eternal condemnation, this His eternal plan for those he loved first. This is proven and I quote Jesus' prayer in Gethsemane, Matthew 26:39 (GNB)

"He went a little farther on, threw himself face downward on the ground, and prayed, "My Father, if it is possible, take this

cup of suffering from me! Yet not what I want, but what you want".

God's will on that night, took precedence over Jesus' request, he died the next day as the ultimate sacrifice for the remission of sin for humankind.

Does sin stand in the way of the answer?

The next question about sin standing in the way of answered prayer, has a bi-poled answer.

On the one hand God hates sin, on the other God loves the sinner. Thus, the answer lies with grace and judgement. Grace is for repentance, and judgement for the unrepented. Will believers be judged for their sin post accepting Christ as their saviour, I believe so because we have an advocate Jesus Christ at the right hand of the Father in heaven who pleads the case of the believer.

Yet, whilst a believer is sinning and not concerned about repenting, in other words backslidden, their prayers may not be sincere enough to be answered by God, He sees the attitude, desire and agenda of the heart or mind.

On the other hand, a backslidden child of God, in an emergency prays because he/she knows only God can help them, their prayers will be answered because God is the God who answers anyone who calls on his name. God's grace is so great, and I quote what Jesus writes to a Church in Laodicea even though he regards them backslidden and lukewarm Revelation 3:19 -20 (GNB)

"I rebuke and punish all whom I love. Be in earnest, then, and turn from your sins.

Listen! I stand at the door and knock; if any hear my voice and open the door, I will come into their house and eat with them, and they will eat with me".

Often people ask me to define sin because there are so many ways of pointing out sin, I have a simple definition that could bring much of what you do wrong to mind. Sin is ultimately working against the will of God through the body, mind, or spirit. It was rooted in the disobedience of Adam and Eve where they damaged their relationship with God by going against His will in the garden of Eden where they did not only bring the curse of death upon themselves but on all humans after them.

Back to my definition of sin for those born into the second Adam, Jesus Christ. 2Corinthians 6:15 -16 (GNB)

"How can Christ and the Devil agree? What does a believer have in common with an

unbeliever? How can God's temple come to terms with pagan idols? For we are the temple of the living God! As God himself has said, "I will make my home with my people and live among them; I will be their God, and they shall be my people".

Consequently, if we are the living temples of God, where God lives amongst His people, and he hates sin then I purport the following definition for it. Sin is an act of disobedience to God through the willful harming of the temple of God, whether it be to one's body, mind, spirit, marriage, family, or the kingdom of God. Moreover, God forgives sin, however the acts of sin bear consequences, which after God's forgiveness, one may still live with the undesired.

Now for the answer, does sin stand in the way of answered prayer, yes, get it out of the way by repenting to God, then your prayers will be answered. I confirm by implication and by quoting Jesus when healing the sick, a paralysed man in Mark 2:8 & 9 (GNB)

"At once Jesus knew what they were thinking, so he said to them, "Why do you think such things? Is it easier to say to this paralyzed man, 'Your sins are forgiven,' or to say, 'Get up, pick up your mat, and walk'?".

The intended answer: for personal glory or for God's?

There is a very important fact about prayer and the answering of prayer concerning honour and glory. Going back to the model prayer of Jesus we find that the opening of the prayer in Matthew 6:9, it honours God's name, then in the closing line it also encapsulates the honour of God again in Matthew 6:13(b) (KJV)

"For thine is the kingdom, and the power, and the glory, forever. Amen".

The glory, at the moment of a miracle, often takes the focus away from God to the instrument of God, who prayed for the miracle to happen. God never intended his children to take His honour, not even Jesus did, he honoured his Father in every prayer he prayed on earth.

Thus, I recommend, that when expecting God to do miracles through us, one takes away pride and stands humble before God. This is done by giving God glory, honour, and praise by allowing those who see the miracles happen, to glorify God for what takes place. There is a very fine line between taking on the glory of the moment for oneself, and the glory that God deserves.

The question that comes to mind is, if one robs God of the honour of the moment, will

God continue working through one? I have two answers here, one is that boasting about one's spiritual power is as dangerous as not having spiritual power at all. Matthew 7:22&23 (KJV) accounts for this

"Many will say to me in that day, Lord, Lord, have we not prophesied in thy name? and in thy name have cast out devils? and in thy name done many wonderful works? And then will I profess unto them, I never knew you: depart from me, ye that work iniquity"

Two, where the first answer was rather aggressive, this one points to the relationship between oneself and God.

In this answer, one is often humbled by God not answering every prayer exactly the way we expect or want. I have this theory that God works through the instruments, his children, who give Him the glory and honour for the works of faith in and for the kingdom of God.

Does God intend answering the prayer later?

Whilst God has the bigger picture of past, present and future, and taking on the role of "Abba", the Hebrew word for Father, one needs to build perspective around God's personal identity with his children. When a child asks his/her father for something, there is an immediate expectation that the request will be heard and acted on. Yet, from the father's side there is a reciprocating expectation that the child would respect the good judgement of his/her parent to do what is best. A good father will however listen, evaluate the request, measure any risk associated, look at the affordability, and adjust the timing of his answer in the interest of his child. Hitherto, the father is fair and objective and may ask his child to wait and make him/her understand that there is a solution and that what was requested will be answered in good time.

Conversely, the child has an expectation that the father has the right to evaluate the request, yet he/she also has faith in the father to know and be almost one hundred percent sure, that the father will not let him/her down.

The child, in most cases, has patience to wait for the positive action of the father, the solution to the child's problem.

With this analogy, one gets a clearer picture of why God does not always answer prayer based on our timing, but on the supernatural, where a God given moment brings change to an earthly situation. Here I relate to my late mother's wise words "the Lord will always give you what you ask for, yet not when you expect it, sometimes much later".

Does God not see my faith?

When one contemplates on one's faith, one should be drawn to the mirror of outcome. Faith is not only the way we believe in God or answered prayer, but it is how we act out faith so that we capitilise on it to move mountains. Again, God's view of us is three dimensional and the view we take of ourselves is two dimensional, as in a mirror.

God's three-dimensional view is spirit, mind, and body, in relation to our view of mostly body and mind. Consequently, the evaluation of one's faith will be put to a spiritual test in a dimension, with a full evaluation of the mind and the actions of the body. The added dimension of faith, the spiritual, will be exemplified by what is clouded around the mind of the individual in relation to believing how God can resolve a matter.

Faith is about believing in the unknown, untouched, unthinkable and in some cases unscientific ways in which solutions can be brought to life by God himself. This belief system is apportioned to the mind and spirit of believers, wherein God is glorified as the creator and master of their lives.

Therefore, God does not only see what faith one has, herewith I consider God's evaluation of the believer's faith to be more spiritual than carnal, and in a sense one's faith speaks directly to God's heart. The more one believes in God's miraculous intervention, the more it will happen as one's spirit is enlightened by the faith contained in the mind. The knowledge of God's powerful interventions, housed in one's conscious and sub-conscious mind, is elevated to the spiritual dimension ensuring that one knows, when God is asked to intervene, it shall be done.

Does the faith of the person prayed for, affect the answer?

A more complex problem one encounters, is when one's prayer of faith is overshadowed by the doubt of another. It is probably easy to say that if a person one prays for does not believe in what is being requested, then the prayer will probably go unanswered. Despite this, it would mean that the believer could not pray for unbelievers, as their faith would probably be non-existent. It is thus safer to say that the faith of the believer will make a difference on outcome for the believer and the unbeliever. However, this does not mean that the person one prays for should not have faith, in some cases the request to God in prayer request of the believer may be denied due to the faithlessness of the person being prayed for.

Let us go back to Peter at the temple in the New testament Church in about AD 33-35. The quoted scripture speaks directly to the actions of the believer and not the unbeliever: Acts 3:6-8

"Then Peter said, Silver and gold have I none; but such as I have give I thee: In the name of Jesus Christ of Nazareth rise up and walk. And he took him by the right hand and lifted him up: and immediately his feet and ankle bones received strength. And he leaping up stood, and walked, and entered with them into the temple, walking, and leaping, and praising God".

The unbeliever was awaiting a carnal gift of money which, naturally, suited his current lifestyle and expectation. Yet, the Peter, filled with the Spirit if God, did not hesitate when it was time to bring healing, in fact this was not even prayer but an act of faith. He did not wait for a response, he took the beggar by the hand and lifted him up, as an action of his own faith, and not the faith of recipient of the miracle.

I therefore appeal to the believer to not be too concerned about the faith of the person being prayed for, but to strengthen the knowledge that God moves when we act out our faith. The reciprocating faith between the person being prayed for and the person praying, will only strengthen the outcome. Yet, I sincerely propose that God will not bring down that standard of faith of one who really believes to that of unbelief and to stop a prayer from being answered.

However, not all prayers are answered immediately and for this reason I purport, that it is not the faith or disbelief of the one praying but God's will and timing that may delay the answer.

Does God put the prayers of others before mine?

When answering this question, one should not equate God to human intelligence or judgement. However, the discussion around this topic is relevant and important. The entire book of Job relates in some way or another, to trying to understand the fair judgement of God back down to the individual.

Because God is fair, and because He loves everyone, each sincere prayer is heard without any petty human complications. Notwithstanding my comments on God's fairness to each individual matter brought to God in prayer, I sketch a scenario which was shared with me years ago by a Pastor in the Western Cape.

In his congregation he had both wheat and wine farmers, both dependent on seasonal harvesting and planting with an opposite rainfall expectation. The wheat farmers were paying for rain, at the same time the grape harvest would be damaged by the same rain. This resulted in two opposing prayers, one for much needed rain and the other for a much-needed harvest of grapes without rain. The reason being that too much water dilutes the juice of the grape, has disease flourish and grapes burst.

Both these prayers are equally important, both have valid substance and both prayers come from children of God and the farmer's farms border on one another.

Taking on the sketched scenario, with human judgement and capability, it may be said that one cannot please everyone at the same time. From God's viewpoint, he can suit both the farmers requirements as each brought before Him their own sincere cause. My theory is this, God is extremely fair, he gave Solomon only a little of his wisdom, and there was none wiser than he. God, I believe analyses and develops a win-win situation for each opposing prayer according to His will and to His glory. Is it then impossible for God, who has the power to give or withhold rain, to have it rain on one farm for purpose and to withhold the same from another for an opposing purpose? The answer is yes, God can answer both prayers and can treat each individual prayer with heavenly care and discretion.

In concluding on the topic of unanswered prayer, I would like to reach into the depths of human intelligence and wisdom wherein one juxtaposes the sincerity of prayer with Godly intervention and purpose. Prayer is the vehicle not for magic, but for miracles, however great or insignificant to others.

Every prayer shapes an outcome, it may not be the one that was expected, yet it will be answered in a way that suites God's bigger picture which includes the molecular makeup, the positioning and purpose, the plan with society and that world region of the individual.

Consequently, even the unanswered prayer has purpose in the greater scheme of things, one may not know why now but it will become evident later. When contemplating about unanswered prayer one needs to reason systematically with context. For this I have several questions you should answer in detail so that you can even assist others who experience unanswered prayer.

Assignment on unanswered prayer

1. How do you bring God's will into context with your prayer and requests?
2. However confidential, do you have something that is standing in the way of your prayer being answered, your spiritual success and or your marriage?
3. How will you advise others on sin and unanswered prayer?
4. How will you relate personal glory to prayer failure?
5. Do you pray about the future, and if so, how do you relate to God's answers to such prayer?
6. How would you explain God's timing to another person who is distressed about unanswered prayer?
7. How would you approach faith if a person really believed that God would have

answered the prayer, and why would you use such an approach?

8. Give your opinion based on scripture whether the faith of the person I am praying for affects the answer?
9. Explain God's righteousness in relation to prayer, also relate to his fair judgement on human matters.

CHAPTER 9

Prayer is not a Ritual

The most condescending way to speak about prayer, is when it becomes a way of proving piousness to others. In other words, "I pray so many times per day". Similarly, if prayers may have become some sort of meaningless recital of someone else's written of recited works, this could even be the Our Father, Hail Mary, table grace and so on. These will not release the power which prayer dialogue with God brings into play, these are boring bubbles of words.

And by saying this I do not imply that poems and written prayers do not have or add spiritual value, they do. Yet if the same thing is said fifty times over in one prayer session, in my opinion, God heard the first version, do we really put God that low to see him having us ask the same thing over and over?

The following questions should be asked about rituals:

1. Do rituals have spiritual meaning?
2. At what stage does a prayer become a ritual?
3. When are rituals institutionalized?
4. Why should prayer not become a ritual?

To this end I apply the definition of a ritual to the debate that follows:

The Oxford Dictionary describes the noun "ritual" as: "*a religious or solemn ceremony consisting of a series of actions performed according to a prescribed order*".

Do rituals have spiritual meaning?

Through Centuries rituals have been adapted and adopted so that the mind of the churchgoer can be satisfied that he or she has salvation from their committed sin. It is obvious for the start of Genesis where the fist sin was committed, and shame caused Adam to hide from God, that human nature is ashamed of wrongdoing. Instead of praying and asking for forgiveness as the Bible teaches, Church leaders often revert to a legalistic system that ascribes to punishment for wrongdoing and reward for good works.

This is where rituals become meaningful and the blood of Christ, which washes away sin is forgotten. The writer of Hebrews says in Chapter 9:25-28 (GNB)

"The Jewish high priest goes into the Most Holy Place every year with the blood of an animal. But Christ did not go in to offer himself many times, for then he would have had to suffer many times ever since the creation of the world. Instead, now when all ages of time are nearing the end, he has appeared once and for all, to remove sin through the sacrifice of himself. Everyone must die once, and after that be judged by God. In the same manner Christ also was offered in sacrifice once to take away the sins of many. He will appear a second time, not to deal with sin, but to save those who are waiting for him".

The High Priest annual ritual was important for atonement of the Jewish nation and had liturgical value and meaning. This did have a very pertinent spiritual meaning for an Israelite, even though they were divided in their principles about life after death. Pharisees believed there was life after death and that after the third day the spirit of the dead depart to paradise of punishment, whilst the Sadducees did not believe in life after death.

In my debate on rituals, I would purport that when Jesus died the spiritual meaning of rituals for cleansing of the soul was annulled. However, there are beneficial rituals which if termed so can be listed as: Baptism, Holy communion, Tithing, Grace at meals, and Marriage, all instituted by God or Jesus his son.

The problem comes when man made rituals are pre-conceived to order salvation or the answer to prayer. Some have even resorted to prayer rituals such as whipping oneself or instituting prayer rituals of many kinds: sack and ash, head coverings, prayer shawls, prayer letters, removing shoes and even closing one's eyes to pray. These prayer rituals are all done with good intention, nonetheless these may not be equal to a pure heart, which God desires from us.

This prayer rituals probably cause a feeling of humility and respect before God, but in my opinion, rituals do not have enough spiritual meaning to change God's mind about the individual. It is the heart or mind of the individual with a clear conscience that has the meaning, notwithstanding the faith one has for the answer to what is being prayed about. Prayer should not become a ritual, it should remain an open communication between God and his children.

At what stage does a prayer become a ritual?

I am going to use a rather common place where prayer has become a ritual, this at the table as we sit down to enjoy a meal. Most Christians still say grace, and most probably a very well organised piece of poetry taught by grandma or mom in the early days of childhood. This is a ritual of thanks because it is recited without the one praying, or those listening, understanding of relating to the prayer that is being recited.

Is saying grace important? It is, however, just maybe because its so watered down it may not bring the blessing asked of God over the food that is about to be consumed. Saying grace should be a fresh prayer of blessing every time.

A second example, and for those who love the Lord's prayer, I do too and have used it in my prayer modelling earlier in the book. Nevertheless, the Lord's prayer can be recited as a ritual by a thousand people at ones and only those who pray it in earnest truth will have a prayerful experience. The ritual of the "our father" is a mere lip service.

When are rituals institutionalized?

Rituals are institutionalized when they become part of the Liturgy in a Church or Congregation. Such rituals become part and parcel of how the service is delivered by the Pastor or Church leader. There are liturgical preferences and normally well formulated in dogmatic directives handed down from a senate or governing body. I do propose that church services need to be professional and well organised, yet I caution that ritualizing a Church service, will not result in the prayers being answered.

In my years of experience as a Pastor, I have learned that a new idea or an innovative change in the style of worship breaks monotony.

Equally however, I have found that a good change that was instituted, and has been seen to work, gets placed in the Liturgical process and becomes "the way we do Church here". Once the change is adopted by the broader community it becomes easy to institutionalize the method and it becomes a ritual.

Why should prayer not become a ritual?

Let us take a journey back to the beginning when God created Adam to be his friend, before disobedience and sin came into play. If one analyses Genesis 3:8 & 9 (KJV)

"And they heard the voice of the LORD God walking in the garden in the cool of the day: and Adam and his wife hid themselves from the presence of the LORD God amongst the trees of the garden. And the LORD God called unto Adam, and said unto him, Where art thou?".

This event took place after Adam and Eve sinned; however, it is implied that God had walked and talked with them daily, and that from the beginning they had been used to the presence of God.

Thus, walking with God daily, would have given Adam and Eve insight into God's will, and it was so because they themselves did not know evil until they brought it upon themselves through the disobedience. Secondly, in the analysis, God's presence is known as a period of dialogue, as God calls out to Adam. Because God was with them in the garden, it seems like God had chosen the picturesque time of sunset to accompany his friends in the garden, implied by the "cool of the day", correspondingly though, it could have been both early morning and evening.

I have used this analysis as basis of my reasoning, that God instituted dialogue with the human being as early as the garden of Eden and then continued visiting those he loved, Cain and Abel the sons of Adam and Eve.

However, interestingly Enoch was the first to really walk with God, so much so that Genesis 5:24 says that God took him to himself, proving that God wants his creation to walk, and by implication, have a personal relationship with Him. From this time onward, God has relationships with Noah, Abraham, Isaac, Jacob, Moses, Samson, David, Solomon, all the prophets, and even more so Samuel, Elijah, Elisha, and Daniel.

Where one can go wrong with prayer is when it is seen as a tick in the box exercise for the day, whereas it should be a time of conversation with God. Jesus' life on earth is a perfect example of how the conversation should be. I have spent much time on this matter in the previous chapters, yet I point out the kind of conversational prayer Jesus has with His father in John 17, his High Priestly prayer before the crucifixion. This prayer is probably the deepest and most respectful prayers prayed for the future of the Church.

Whilst ceremonial prayer or opening prayer at functions or services is important as a communal act to respect God and to ask God to bless the event, the conversational prayer of the individual is more important.

This leads to another question, is it wrong to write a prayer before praying it? Absolutely not, nonetheless if this written prayer is read and recited over and over as a ritual it shall lose its meaning and transpose into a lost prayer that does not come from the heart and probably does not reach God as it should. However, prayers and recitals do have their place and can bring about an anointing when one enters God's presence with a culmination of praise and worship.

Maybe I should discuss repetitive recitals of prayers for forgiveness or penance. Do these rituals work, and will one eventually be forgiven after the hard and fast rule has been complied with?

On this matter of institutionalized forgiveness, one goes back to religious laws and rules that satisfy human ego and dominance. With all due respect to God, is He so boring that he would sit in heaven and wait to hear 15 million of the same recitals per day? Or would our Father in heaven rather hear about what really matters in the heart of his children? I propose the latter would be what constitutes a personal relationship, and the former question's answer, an institutionalized ritual with no power, leaving individuals to be drawn along as puppets of a human empire of dead worship, rather than a dialogue of true feelings and sincere devotion.

Are those who do rituals for forgiveness wrong and undedicated? This question I seek to answer with a subsequent question, who gave humanity forgiveness through the ultimate price of life, on the cross of Calvary? Was it not the God's Son, Jesus Christ? Likewise, have all not sinned? I quote Romans 3:23 -26 (GNB)

"For all have sinned and come short of the glory of God; Being justified freely by his grace through the redemption that is in Christ Jesus: Whom God hath set forth to be a propitiation through faith in his blood, to declare his righteousness for the remission of sins that are past, through the forbearance of God. To declare, I say, at this time his righteousness: that he might be just, and the justifier of him which believeth in Jesus".

Moreover, it is repentance, grace, forgiveness, or remission, and then freedom, in this order. Repentance is an individual act of regret that is pardoned by the grace of God through Jesus Christ our saviour. The freedom of sin requires no further ritual of recitals for forgiveness, however a humble heart with regret moves the mind to freedom through the grace of God with no penance or payment due.

In summary if prayer becomes a ritual, it will lose its meaning and its heavenly connection. God wants to communicate with His children through the third person in the trinity, the Holy Spirit. Likewise, God wants his children to communicate with him in a father child relationship. This dialogue is done by faith to the unseen, omnipotent

God, who is omnipresent through and by his Holy Spirit.

True freedom of the conscious and subconscious mind by the cleansing from sin, is unique to Christianity. Being freed from sin, allows God's children to use prayer as the vehicle for heavenly conversation without institutionalized recitals and rituals. It is not how much or how long one prays; it is the quality of the conversation with God that will make the difference.

This is a short assignment to ensure that one does not fall into the trap of prayer rituals.

Assignment Prayer and rituals

1. How would you explain to someone that prayer repetition has very little purpose?
2. Does reciting a prayer poem over and over as a punishment allow for forgiveness of sin? If not explain why?
3. How does the cleansing of sin take place in the conscious and subconscious mind?
4. Do you think saying grace is a ritual? if so, how would you change the prayer?
5. Explain the works of conversing with God in relation to doing prayer rituals.

CHAPTER 10 - Revival and prayer

From the outset of this chapter, I want to make it clear, by definition, that Church growth is not necessarily Church revival. Church growth programmes call for filling churches, targeting the un-Churched. Therefore, Church growth is a fundamental outcome through acts of discipleship, leadership, prayer, cell groups, church management, facilities, programmes, human behavior, training, gifting, advertising, and a universal theology for a broader spectrum of the populace [11].

Revival on the other hand has to do with the Holy Spirit and the Church. The world-wide revivals that had taken place, were interconnected with fervent prayer, the works of the Holy Spirit, "hell-fire" preaching, sinners repenting, societal change and the like. These revivals were not happening in comfortable auditoriums or churches but were in open air meetings, cold and uncomfortable tents and in house churches [12] [13] [14] [15] [16].

As much as Church growth is extremely important and is a direct action of the great commandment of Christ, one cannot equate it to revival. As revival is brought about through the dynamics of the prayer, waves of the Holy Spirit movement, spiritual warfare, and God's timing. In summary, revival requires the spiritual acts of the Church where Church growth is mostly about the management of spiritual welfare of people, facilities, and Church programmes [17] [18] [19].

Throughout the history of the Church a necessity for revival was paramount to wake the Church and take it back to the fundamentals of the Gospel: discipleship, the fivefold ministry, prayer, and faith in action. Such revival or Church awakenings were indicative of repentance, prayer and supplication of a group or groups of believers who sought the deeper meaning of gospel foundations through the guidance of the Holy Spirit. Countless testimonies from revival periods from the 18th Century point to all night prayer meetings, intercession, calls for sanctification, and un-staged miracles [20].

I do however stress the fact that revival is probably the greater source of Church growth, but it does not come overnight. As the Church awaits a last revival before the coming of Christ, several fundamental questions need to be answered namely:

1. Is waiting for revival enough?
2. Why sanctification before revival?
3. What are keys to revival?
4. Can the individual call for revival of the Church?
5. How does the Church opt for revival?

6. Who rebuilds the prayer altar in the Church?

I will attempt to answer each of these questions in line with an expectation that I carry in my heart for a Holy Spirit Revival which will not be for a denomination, province, state, or country but for the millennial Church and body of Christ.

Is waiting for revival enough?

Whilst true revival is a sign of turning back to the roots of the Christian Church: taking back the Holy Spirit, piousness, acts of faith and preaching the Gospel of Christ without theological interference, an expectation of greater spiritual awakening exists in the Church.

As the climate of spiritual change comes from the Holy Spirit, the comforter sent to us from heaven, the Church needs to know that it has never been withdrawn from the Church, but rather shut-out many a time.

From the records in history about revival, it appears that it either comes by a group of people who anticipate a visit from God and who prepare for such by the cleansing of the inner man/woman knowing that God can only work through clean and holy people. Yet, an expectation for revival is centered around those who have heard from God, they believe that He is going to work through the Holy Spirit.

Going as far back as the Acts 1, one sees that a 120 were in anticipation of a visitation from God, they were prepared to wait on the Lord in the upper room in Jerusalem. The writer of Acts gives account of this in Acts 1:3 - 5 "For forty days after his death he (Jesus) appeared to them many times in ways that proved beyond doubt that he was alive. They saw him, and he talked with them about the Kingdom of

God. And when they came together, he gave them this order: (GNB)

"*Do not leave Jerusalem, but wait for the gift I told you about, the gift my Father promised. John baptized with water, but in a few days, you will be baptized with the Holy Spirit.*"

The same as the waiting period as in scripture it can be noted that [(21)] many evangelical revivals started with prayer. The outpouring of the Holy Spirit has been evident not only in the speaking of tongues but with crying, laughter and been seen to be drunk in of the Spirit. It has been cited that [(21)] revival is a product of correct planting of seed where a harvest is expected. Thus, revival will not come only through waiting on God.

It will come when unity in prayer, sanctification, preaching, discipleship, and expectation of such in supplication to God.

In other words, the soil should be prepared, seed sown and then watered with and expectation of a harvest called revival.

Why sanctification before revival?

Sanctification, the way to holiness, to which a Christian is called to is a direct act following salvation, not doing the sin as before but cleaning up the body mind and spirit. One cannot expect revival when the spiritual machinery is out of order, or when the leaders do not channel the order of God but rather their own. Just as the proverb says the fish rots from the head, so conversely too revival starts when the leaders are guided and set on pleasing God in everything they do.

The possible problem in the post millennial church is that God's love is preached in such a way that it is so motivational that the believer and the unbeliever feel comfortable with being lukewarm. Sanctification, however, calls for the sharpening of the two-edged sword which should convict the minds of Christians to do right all the time, within the will of God. Progressing to a state of holiness is what God wants of His children and having a kingdom full of lukewarm believers constitutes a lukewarm church.

Revelation 3:15-18 speaks very clearly to the condition of the post millennial church. I quote, (GNB)

"I know what you have done; I know that you are neither cold nor hot. How I wish you were either one or the other! But because you are lukewarm, neither hot nor cold, I am going to spit you out of my mouth! You say, 'I am rich and well off; I have all I need.' But you do not know how miserable and

pitiful you are! You are poor, naked, and blind."

In a state of comfortability revival will not be possible, sanctification means dedication of every moment to God, whether asleep or awake. Is this possible? Absolutely, God does not expect anything of us that his Son did not do on earth. Jesus lived a dedicated, sanctified life on earth doing the will of his Father throughout, even in his early years before his ministry began, sanctification was his way of life. So too sanctification should become the way of life for a believer after salvation, the question is, do we as the Church teach new-born believers this fundamental practice or not?

Thus, in answering why sanctification comes before revival, one cannot have revival whilst the ground is not dedicated to it. Thus, once the core ministry is sanctified, dedicated to the principle of revival, the process to enact it has started. Prayer is a tool for sanctification [22].

What are keys to revival?

My perspective on the quest for revival will pivot off seven specific keys.

1st Key, a passion for prayer. Without prayer and the belief in what is being prayed for, the cause for revival is probably not clear. Born again believers should be taught how to pray from the outset.

To clarify the misunderstanding of the two parts of the great commission, I quote Matthew 28:19&20 (GNB)"Go, then, to all peoples everywhere and make them my disciples: baptize them in the name of the Father, the Son, and the Holy Spirit, and teach them to obey everything I have commanded you. And I will be with you always, to the end of the age". Clearly, after making disciples a teaching process should follow, this includes teaching them to pray.

2nd Key to revival is looking at the indicators in the mission of the Church.

1. Are congregants taught to pray out loud and to worship God even in tongues?
2. Are the members actively involved in prayer meetings, prayer rooms, prayer groups or all-night prayer relays?
3. Are the cell groups praying and studying the Bible, or are they merely social get-togethers?
4. Is repentance and sanctification part and parcel of the Sunday sermons?
5. Are the congregants taught about the Holy Spirit, its gifts, and are the gifts of the Spirit allowed to operate in the Church service?
6. Are there souls being saved with follow-up gatherings for teaching and clarification?

7. Is there an expectation for a visit of his Holy Spirit, at each meeting?

3rd Key, our Holy Bible, where believers anticipate the filling of spiritual voids by reading and understanding the word of God. Most post-millennial believers rely on media to tell them about God's word, rather than them reading and believing it for themselves. The active reading of the Bible should culminate in the quotation of scripture in prayer.

4th Key, an anticipation for the second coming of Christ, inclusive of the prophetic, Jesus's teachings in the gospels, the New Testament Letters and Revelation.

5th Key, the number of people being baptized into the body of Christ, as a prevalent as part of the ministry.

6th Key, the amount of time spent on waiting for God's will, over important Church matters and decisions.

7th Key, advertising, and marketing revival, as a return to Biblical principles and the Acts of the Church as Jesus wants it to be.

Can the individual call for revival of the Church?

If one looks back at the history of revivals, most originated at the call of one person who was so dedicated to God that his/her message of the Gospel propelled revival. After all it is the anointing of God, by the Holy Spirit, that drives the quest for revival and revival campaigns.

A revival can be born in a woman or man of God through total dedication to the works of divine intervention. Revival can be an Apostolic, Prophetic of evangelistic calling but will not come to fruition until God releases the spiritual rain. The release of the revival wave should most probably come through the individual who is dedicated to purpose, agile enough to change direction when God commands, having an anointing of God, and a keen ear to hear God's voice.

I do however repeat that revival is preceded by prayer, fasting, sanctification, supplication, and humility of an individual that seeks to do God's will. The individual that seeks God's will, leads by example, has a vison for revival and lives a blameless life, can pronounce a revival in the Church. He/she can lead such a campaign through hard work, organisation, an apostolic mission. An anointing of the Holy Spirit to do miracles, to discern, and to do the works of faith will be eminent as a forerunner of revival.

How does the Church opt for revival?

Opting for a discourse on revival will be the choice and prerogative of the visionary leader of the church. Because revival is not an instantaneous precipitation of the Holy Spirit, but an extension of a preparation time, the harvest of what was sown in this period.

Utilising the Pareto principle, "80% of consequences come from 20% of the causes (23)" would mean that if a pastor could get a mere 20% of his/her congregation to become involved in the revival mission, a further 80% of the congregation would be drawn into the vision by the momentum of revival created by the eager starters.

The momentum for revival will be caused by a pre-supposed order of prayer though the internal circle of four or five individuals taking lead in prayer activities, charters, timetables, and venues. The entire startup operation should be such that it does not come with an administration burden, it should be action based with as little paper involves as possible. Prayer times and commitment is what is required not record keeping.

Prayer lines, topics, requests, and the like should become prominent and these activities may include prayer walks, intercession, spiritual warfare, prayer zoning, hotspot identification and the like. The church or congregation need to understand that prayer is the seed sown for the harvest of revival.

Who rebuilds the prayer altar in the Church?

As an altar of stone was built under the leadership of the High Priest and Priesthood in the days of Moses, so too the leadership of the Church under the blessing of the visionary leader, or pastor, is responsible for the rebuilding of the prayer altar in his/her church.

It is about teaching believers that to be in the presence of the Lord is not only a Church occasion. Prayer is one of the most important acts of a believer and cements his/her relationship with God through the Holy Spirit.

The prayer altar of the Church is a communal altar, as important as the communal celebration of the body of Christ with Holy Communion. The prayer altar signifies the spiritual strength of the congregation and ensures that the body of believers can pray together with faith that their prayers will be answered.

Elijah took a bold step by rebuilding the altar of God from scratch in the wake of his payer that brought fire from heaven. A simple prayer, an act of faith which brought about a miraculous moment of divine intervention.

It is the boldest step that a church leader can take, the rebuilding of the prayer altar in the church will bring great spiritual and carnal reward. Prayer altars are not physical one made of stone, they are ones built with believers who unite in prayer for the cause of Christ, to intercede for the lost, to do spiritual warfare and create a dimension for miracles and healing in the Church.

Will all go well in the Church when the prayer altar is restored? The answer is no, firstly the altar will need to be maintained else it will stop functioning. Secondly, not all who start the race will see it through, there will always be those who get discouraged and give up on prayer.

Finally, the prayer altar attracts the enemy, Satan's attention, he knows the power of the believer's prayer and he will try to destroy the spiritual harmony of the prayer altar.

This should not discourage one because the prayer altar come with the full authority of Christ.

As most believers look forward to revival and pastors set up such campaigns regularly to enhance church growth, one needs to plan and decide what revival really is and means to the Church.

Assignment: Revival and Action

1. Is waiting for revival worth waiting for or are actions required, if so, what would these be?
2. Why is sanctification important and how can it be related to personal life, family, work, and society at large?
3. Explain the seven keys to revival and how you would use them to start a revival campaign.
4. Can the individual call for revival of the Church, could you spark off a revival if so, how do you see this happening?
5. As a visionary leader, how will you get your church to opt for a revival strategy and by what means?
6. What strategies would you use to rebuild the prayer altar in the Church?
7. If you were asked to produce a revival plan on one page, what would the seven strategies be and how will you get

everyone to understand it, remember "Less say More".

8. Build an ideal marketing statement for your revival campaign not using more than five words.
9. Set up an agenda for your revival planning meeting and list the people you will invite and why?
10. How do you intend using social media as a platform for the campaign?

CHAPTER 11 - When God moves

As the final chapter of this book, I would like to attribute it to a move of God. This is a topic that can span over light years into eternity, and I shall endeavor to scrape the surface of God's power and movement through human prayer and communication with Him.

To ringfence the discussion on the movement of God I would like to address two matters: one, divine intervention in a personal and individual capacity, and two, the divine intervention in the Church of Christ which I touched on in the Chapter on Revival.

I will start with a righteous man, Job's view on God's plan for the individual and I quote Job 23:12-14 (GNB)

"I always do what God commands; I follow his will, not my own desires. He never changes. No one can oppose him or stop him from doing what he wants to do. He will fulfill what he has planned for me; that plan is just one of the many he has".

There are numerous ways in which God moves visibly and invisibly for the believer. I list seven ways in which God moves for further discussion:

1. As Creator
2. As Provider
3. As Revelator
4. As Saviour
5. As Healer
6. In Presence
7. Through eternity

I wish to dedicate this last chapter to the one who created, loved, saved, He who gave us eternal life, the Holy one, our Father in heaven through His Son, who sits on His right hand and who guides us by the Holy Spirt who dwells in and amongst us. Each descriptive aspect of God or the Godhead has relevance to the believer, their understanding of God and how God works in and around them.

As Creator

As creator God has moved from outside of known time into four stages of the earth, pre-Adamite, the creation of the world and life, the human dispensation, lastly the destruction and re-creation of the world. One only seems to concentrate on the creation of the world in Genesis, yet the understanding of the creation and the existence of the universe is also in the domain of God as creator. However, our minds are limited to our earthly habitat and one stands amazed at the expanse of the unknown, even the promise of the new heaven and earth as recorded in Revelation as the new Jerusalem where the sun's rays will no longer be required for light.

I believe that God has never stopped creating and what so astounding is that God created echo-systems that maintain and sustain themselves. God is proud of his creation, although humanity has disappointed him over and over, in the recorded 6 000 years of their existence.

The vast expanse of the universe is inhabited by God and the Angelic. However, what is more incredible is that the creator has the entire expanse of the universe in his care, yet he nurtures his footstool, earth, the world we live in. As part of God's creation, we can communicate with the Father through the Son. Whilst God and his whereabouts in the universe is not known to man of science, God can do anything on earth through his creative power.

Thus prayer, is the only way in which we can communicate with God at an unaccountable speed. The loving relationship between God and man, his creation lives on through eternity as humans receive grace to live on through eternity by the life-giving salvation acquired on the cross of calvary.

Prophetically God speaks as creator in Isaiah 45:7 & 48 (GNB)

"I create both light and darkness; I bring both blessing and disaster. I, the LORD, do all these things. I will send victory from the sky like rain; the earth will open to receive it and will blossom with freedom and justice. I, the LORD, will make this happen".

The creative power of God is available throughout the earth at the mention of Jesus' name in as faith is put into action.

The interesting part of creation is that God

commanded, and it was so. The creation power is thus spoken by God from heaven as in the creation days when God said let there be light, and planets shifted to enable day and night to occur. Thus, we have an expectation of God's the spoken creative word, that, is as powerful force in life though our prayers reaching heaven. In closing on this argument, I allege that the very existence of the believer and his/her surroundings is due to the spoken creative word of God. The believer receives creative talents or power from God through faith and prayer.

As Provider

To call on God as provider is a privilege that one has received through the acceptance of Jesus Christ as saviour and joining the kingdom of God. The origin of the word "Jehovah jireh", God will provide, dates back to Abraham when he went to offer

Isaac, and instead God provided a ram that could be offered. I quote Genesis 22:13&14 (KJV)

"*And Abraham lifted up his eyes, and looked, and behold behind him a ram caught in a thicket by his horns: and Abraham went and took the ram and offered him up for a burnt offering in the stead of his son. And Abraham called the name of that place Jehovah Jireh: as it is said to this day, In the mount of the LORD it shall be seen*".

In this way, one sees that God will provide for his children when they are in need. One can call on the name of the Most-High, anytime day or night, and the call for provision will be heard.

As Revelator

At this point I would like to give God the Father the honour as the revelator of the future. One must realise that our earthly environment and our human make-up does not allow us any visibility of the future, only the present and past. However, through the revelator, the Holy Spirit and by means of the Angelic, God has revealed future events through prophecy and visitation. Such visitations of revelation are well recorded in the Bible, yet not limited to the most well known in Daniel and revelation.

One too sees Jesus speak as the revelator through parables in the Gospels of the New Testament. Revelatory power has been handed down to the Church through the gifts of the Spirit especially, yet not limited to, discernment and prophecy.

It is the power of revelation that the Church can function as a collective in times of trouble and need. The revelatory power of God is shared with the Church through those who earnestly wait on God in prayer and supplication.

As Saviour

As early as Deuteronomy God is referred *to as the savior, also this is confirmed in several Psalms and the climax of the saving grace of God is announce in* John 3:16 &17 and I quote (GNB),

"For God loved the world so much that he gave his only Son, so that everyone who believes in him may not die but have eternal life. For God did not send his Son into the world to be its judge, but to be its savior".

Albeit that God is the God of salvation, such salvation is realised though prayer, the sinner's prayer as commonly termed in the Charismatic and Pentecostal movements. One is obliged to repent of sin to the Father, through the Son Jesus Christ before God changes form the God of Judgement to the God of Grace. This grace allows for a believer's name to be written in the book of life after all his/her sins are forgiven.

As Healer

God is not only the healer of individuals but also of nations. As far back Abraham's prayer for Abimelech where God Healed him (Genesis 20:17-18). Also, in Exodus when the plaques, such as boils and livestock death in Egypt, the Israelites where covered by a healing umbrella, Exodus 8,9 &10. Then a pertinent incident takes place in the

Desert according to Numbers 21:6-9 and I quote (GNB):

"Then the LORD sent poisonous snakes among the people, and many Israelites were bitten and died. The people came to Moses and said, "We sinned when we spoke against the LORD and against you. Now pray to the LORD to take these snakes away."

So, Moses prayed for the people. Then the LORD told Moses to make a metal snake and put it on a pole, so that anyone who was bitten could look at it and be healed. So, Moses made a bronze snake and put it on a pole. Anyone who had been bitten would look at the bronze snake and be healed"

Then in the New Testament the healing power of God is shared with the Church. Healing becomes a sign of the believer through Christ. Christ sends out the disciples to heal the sick and to drive out demons.

At the great commission in Mark 16:16-18 the healing of the sick is transposed onto the believer as an act of grace and a sign that God hears their prayer. Healing, and the prayer for should be undistinguished with the Church of Christ. Healing through Godly intervention is also a gift of the Spirit and is not out of reach of the believer's prayer.

In Presence

A question often asked is, and many works have been published in this regard, is God everywhere, is He omnipresent? And if so, why is it recorded that God and Jesus are not on earth but in a heavenly throne room as described in Matthew, Hebrews, and Revelation. The answer is evident by understanding the Holy Trinity, Father, Son and Holy Spirit. The omnipresence of God is accomplished by the Holy Spirit and the omnipotence of God is manifest all over the earth. The second layer of God's presence, not to well known by believers, is the Angelic protection that is provided on earth for the believer.

God's presence however is felt by a believer or "a group of believers when they gather in God's name. Jesus testifies to this phenomenon in Matthew 18:19 -20 (GNB)

"*Again I say unto you, that if two of you shall agree on earth as touching anything that they shall ask, it shall be done for them of my Father which is in heaven. For where two or three are gathered together in my name, there am I in the midst of them*".

What better example does one want as the outpouring of the Holy Spirit in Acts 2, and the presence of God can be felt in a room when people get together to pray. God is omnipresent where His children get together to worship and pray.

Through eternity

One must understand that God is eternal and undefined, however, God exists outside of time. Unfortunately, believers measure their spiritual activity in an earthly way equated in human years because eternity sounds almost impossible. The believer's relationship with God is an eternal one that was brought about with salvation. Because eternity contradicts death, eternity become a matter of faith. God has promised eternal life, Paradise and heaven are described in the Bible and when believers die, they go to where God is.

What is sure and that is spoken to throughout the New Testament and explained by Jesus is that there is a Paradise, there is a possibility of different levels of heaven. Conversely, to the detriment of the unbeliever God is still the judge of those who do not accept Jesus Christ as the personal saviour. The eternal judgement will be a bottomless pit, a lake of fire or both. Unfortunately, this will also be eternal and a place of torment as it is described in the Bible.

How God works and moves

In summary God sees the past, understands the present and has a full view of the future although it does not exist. The hand of God is always available for movement on request through prayer. Still, God moves over and with the anointed believer for spiritual and moral purpose. The movement of God could emanate from fervent prayer, supplication, and faith in action. Such a move of God cannot be stopped as it comes with creative power, provision, saving grace, revelation, healing, a Godly presence and eternal power and glory.

The radiating power of the almighty God will be felt and comes with signs and wonders. The more the presence of God through his Holy Spirit, the more the functioning of the gifts, the more visible the work of God will become. Such waves that culminate into revival, cannot be stopped by human intervention. History has proven that revival is indicative of supernatural impact.

Epilogue

I have written this book because I long for a Holy Spirit revival, and I have noticed in the last 20 years of active ministry and theological study, that the children of God are not praying as they used to. Nonetheless, I have come to notice that Christians require instant gratification as far as spiritual nourishment is concerned. Unfortunately, there are no ways to be spiritually successful without prayer. To this end this book is published as a functional guide that will empower believers in their prayer journey to spiritual maturity and success.

In closing I implore believers to pray as Jesus prayed and to understand the fundamental basics of prayer. If one prays with purpose, and with faith, I could guarantee God's intervention. One should understand that prayer is work, and likewise fasting is part and parcel of working towards becoming a powerful prayer warrior.

When believers feel their prayers are unanswered it should be open to reasoning so that they do not become despondent. However, the answered prayers will prove that it is worth praying and that fervent prayer is no ritual. Albeit, prayer is the vehicle of revival, calling for the rebuilding of the prayer altar at home and in Church.

Lastly, doing the assessments will enable the reader to take out as much as possible out of the book for spiritual empowerment.

Bibliography

Allen, M. (n.d.). *Pentecostal Movement Celebrates Humble Roots*. Retrieved 12 20, 2020, from https://www.washingtonpost.com/wp-dyn/content/article/2006/04/14/AR2006041401421.html

American Bible Society . (1966, 1967, 1970, 1971, 1976, 1979). *The Good News Bible.* London, UK: Bible Societies, HarperCollins.

American Vegan Society. (2019, 12 16). *What is Vegan?* Retrieved 12 16, 2019, from American Vegan Society: http://www.americanvegan.org/vegan.htm

Authorised King James Version. (2004). *Holy Bible.* Nashville, TN, USA: World Publishing.

Baker, R. (1999). *The Impact of Prayer on the Ministries of D.L. Moody, C.H. Spurgeon, and Billy Graham: A Descriptive Study*. Retrieved 12 21, 2020, from https://digitalcommons.liberty.edu/cgi/viewcontent.cgi?article=1195&context=doctoral

Bloomer, R. J., Kabir, M. M., Trepanowski, J. F., Canale, R. E., & Farney, T. M. (2011). A 21 day Daniel Fast improves selected biomarkers of antioxidant status and oxidative stress in men and women. *Nutrition & Metabolism, 8*(1), 17-17. Retrieved 12 16, 2019, from https://nutritionandmetabolism.biomedcentral.com/track/pdf/10.1186/1743-7075-8-17

Bounds, E. M. (2009). *Power through prayer.* Chicago, USA: Moody Publishers.

Charles, K. (2010). *Wisdom Bible Lesson for Children: Hidden Treasure Proverbs*. Retrieved 3 5, 2020, from https://ministry-to-children.com/wisdom-bible-lesson

Clark, R. (2006). *Fast Facts About Osteoarthritis*. Retrieved 11 23, 2019, from https://niams.nih.gov/health_info/osteoarthritis/osteoarthritis_ff.asp

Craft, R. C., & Leake, C. (2002). The Pareto principle in organizational decision making. *Management Decision, 40*(8), 729-733. Retrieved 12 22, 2020, from https://emerald.com/insight/content/doi/10.1108/00251740210437699/full/html

Dekar, P. R. (1995). Modern Christian Revivals . Edited by Edith L. Blumhofer and Randall Balmer. Urbana: University of Illinois Press, 1993. xviii + 232 pp. $32.50 cloth; $12.95 paper. *Church History, 64*(01), 154-156. Retrieved 12 20, 2020, from https://cambridge.org/core/journals/church-history/article/modern-christian-revivals-edited-by-blumhofer-edith-l-and-balmer-randall-urbana-university-of-illinois-press-1993-xviii-232-pp-3250-cloth-1295-paper/f4bc331a97858f78f031414a46a3185f

Dolphin, L. (2019, 09 05). *World Population Since Creation*. Retrieved from World Population : http://www.ldolphin.org/popul.html

Guzik, D. (2020, 02 13). *On-line Bible Commentary* . Retrieved from Enduring Word: https://enduringword.com/bible-commentary/

Hummel, D. (2016). Revivalist Nationalism since World War II: From "Wake up, America!" to "Make America Great Again". *Religion, 7*(11), 128. Retrieved 12 20, 2020, from https://mdpi.com/2077-1444/7/11/128

Humphreys, C. J., & Waddington, W. G. (1983). Dating the Crucifixion. *Nature, 306*(5945), 743-746. Retrieved 9 3, 2019, from http://adsabs.harvard.edu/abs/1983natur.306..743h

Hutton, J. M. (2011). Just how literal is the King James Version. *Journal of Northwest Semitic Languages, 37*(1), 27-48. Retrieved 9 5, 2019, from https://repository.nwu.ac.za/handle/10394/2924

Jarvis, P. W. (2019, 11 21). *Fasting*. Retrieved 11 22, 2019, from National Council Against Health Fraud: http://www.ncahf.org/articles/e-i/fasting.html

Kim, C. K. (2010). *Biblical Strategy and Shift to Spiritual Driven Church Growth*. Retrieved 12 20, 2020, from https://digitalcommons.liberty.edu/cgi/view content.cgi?article=1355&context=doctoral

King James Bible . (2004). *Standard English version.* Nashvilee, TN, USA: World Publihing.

Knapton, S. (2019, 12 14). *Fasting for three days can regenerate entire immune system, study finds*. Retrieved 12 14, 2019, from The Telegraph: https://www.telegraph.co.uk/news/uknews/10878625/Fasting-for-three-days-can-regenerate-entire-immune-system-study-finds.html

Kocher, C. (2019, 09 17). *An ActionCOACH business coaching blog*. Retrieved from What's Your Formula For Success?: http://actioncoachchuckkocher.com/what%E2%80%99s-your-formula-for-success/

Larson, M. (1950). *Revival In Our Time: The Story of the Billy Graham Evangelistic Campaigns including Six of his Sermons.* Van Kampen Press. Retrieved 12 20, 2020 merriam-webster. (2019, 11 21). *Definition of RITUAL*. Retrieved 11 22, 2019, from merriam-webster: https://www.merriam-webster.com/dictionary/ritual

Olwa, A. (2014). Festo Kivengere, a Ugandan preacher in Australia. *St. Mark's Review*(230), 103. Retrieved 12 20, 2020, from http://search.informit.com.au/fulltext;dn=896740190912337;res=ielhss

Pilz, A. (2014). *60th anniversary of Harringay Crusade*. Retrieved 12 20, 2020, from https://eauk.org/church/stories/harringay-crusade-60th-anniversary.cfm

Porter, J. D. (1991). *An Analysis of Evangelical Revivals with Suggestions for Encouraging and Maximizing the Effects of an Outpouring of the Holy Spirit in Evangelism*. Retrieved 12 21, 2020, from https://digitalcommons.liberty.edu/cgi/viewcontent.cgi?article=1236&context=doctoral

Ransom, M. R., & Alicke, M. D. (2012). It's a Miracle: Separating the Miraculous from the Mundane. *Archive for the Psychology of Religion, 34*(2), 243-275. Retrieved 3 4, 2020, from https://philpapers.org/rec/raniam

Roper, R. (unknown). *EXTRA-BIBLICAL REFERENCES to the Crucifixion.* Unpublished.

Schäfer, T. (1955). Jonathan Edwards' Conception of the Church *. *Church History, 24*(01), 51-66. Retrieved 12 20, 2020, from https://cambridge.org/core/journals/church-history/article/div-classtitlejonathan-edwardsandapos-conception-of-the-churcha-hreffn01-ref-typefnadiv/0c0e20e311e06cec609590623e9cd05b

Schweitzer, D. (2002). Karl Barth's Critique of Classical Theism. *Toronto Journal of Theology, 18*(2), 231-244. Retrieved 9 3, 2019, from https://utpjournals.press/doi/10.3138/tjt.18.2.231

Simpson, J., & Weiner, E. (2013). Oxford English Dictionary: The Definitive Record of the English Language. *Oxford English Dictionary, 1*. Retrieved 3 3, 2020, from http://oed.com

Strong, J. (2009). *Strong's Exhaustive Concordance of the Bible.* Peabody, USA: Hendrickson Publishers, Incorporated.

The Outpouring of the Holy Ghost at Azusa Street Mission. (n.d.). Retrieved 12 20, 2020, from http://www.revempete.us/research/holiness/azusa.html

The Water Page. (2019, 12 11). Retrieved 12 11, 2019, from Water scarcity in Africa:

http://www.thewaterpage.com/live-without-water.htm

United Nations. (2019, 09 04). *World Population*. Retrieved from worldometers: https://www.worldometers.info/world-population/

Wit, J. D., & Theron, J. (2007). *From Hatfield Baptist Church to Hatfield Christian Church : perspectives on some historical developments during the ministry of Pastor Ed Roebert*. Retrieved 12 21, 2020, from http://uir.unisa.ac.za/handle/10500/4466

Yang, S.-y. (2008). A Process View of Wisdom. *Journal of Adult Development, 15*(2), 62-75. Retrieved 3 5, 2020, from https://link.springer.com/article/10.1007/s10804-008-9037-8

[ii] *Origen of Alexandria (182-254 AD), in Against Celsus (Book II, Chap. XIV), wrote that Phlegon, in his "Chronicles", mentions Jesus: "Now Phlegon, in the thirteenth or fourteenth book, I think, of his Chronicles, not only ascribed to Jesus a knowledge of future events (although falling into confusion about some things which refer to Peter, as if they referred to Jesus), but also testified that the result corresponded to His predictions." He referred to a description by Phlegon of an eclipse accompanied by earthquakes during the reign of Tiberius: that there was "the greatest eclipse of the sun" and that "it became night in the sixth hour of the day [i.e., noon] so that stars even appeared in the heavens. There was a great earthquake in Bithynia, and many things were overturned in Nicaea."*